Making Moments Meaningful
in Child & Youth Care Practice

2nd Edition

Edited by
Thom Garfat, Ph.D
Leon C. Fulcher, Ph.D
John Digney, Ph.D

The
CYC-Net
PRESS

THE CYC-NET PRESS

Making Moments Meaningful in Child & Youth Care Practice

Editors
Thom Garfat Ph.D, Leon C. Fulcher Ph.D, John Digney Ph.D

2nd Edition
Copyright © 2019
ISBN 978-0-6399718-1-0

The
CYC-Net
PRESS

An imprint of Pretext Publishing
PO Box 23199, Claremont 7735, Cape Town, South Africa
http://press.cyc-net.org
info@press.cyc-net.org

Readings

Making Moments Meaningful in Daily Life

Welcome to our book about making moments meaningful through the *Purposeful Use of Daily Life Events©*. Welcome to the old, the updated, the revised and the new. We say it like that because the use of daily life events has been around for a long time and is constantly being revisited or updated and new ideas emerge frequently – see, for example the revised version of the Characteristics of a Relational Child & Youth Care Approach (Chapter 2).

We believe that the purposeful use of daily life events, founded in a Child & Youth Care Approach can help to reduce the amount of time many young people, families or others have to live with the current pain in their lives.

The questions which underlay the *The Purposeful Use of Daily Life Events* are these:

- How do we make an everyday life event meaningful for a young person or other?

- How do we make what might otherwise be an ordinary or 'fleeting' moment into something meaningful in terms of reaching the goals we have established together to help reduce the pain in their lives?

- How do we ensure that our best efforts to make a single Moment or event, with this young person is as helpful, healing and purposefully meaningful as it can be?

Those are, in many ways, the ultimate questions for our work – whether we name ourselves as Child and Youth Care Worker, Youth Worker, Social Pedagogue, Social Care Worker or any one of our numerous different titles. If we want to be as effective as we can be and if we want to be as helpful as we can be in assisting a young person or other to move on to a place of less pain and trouble, then we need to wonder about how we can make the most of every moment we have with her or him. After all, the longer it takes, the longer they are in pain.

The articles in this book are intended to 'deepen' your knowledge in the areas of a Child and Youth Care Approach and the Purposeful Use of Daily Life Events. In many ways this book contains less than it could have because there is a wealth of information available to us on the importance and relevance of using daily life events. Much additional information can be found at the International Child and Youth Care Network (https://www.cyc-net.org) from where some of the materials in this book have been drawn.

We encourage you to go there and explore even deeper this aspect of helping troubled young people and their families.

So take your time, read, enjoy and make this reading time a meaningful moment for yourself. After all, meaningful moments are as important for us as for anyone.

Thom, John and Leon

2019

1

The Meaningful Use of Everyday Life Events in Child & Youth Care (Revised)

Thom Garfat

It seems unclear when the expression "the use of everyday life events" first entered the child and youth care literature. Probably, like many things in our field, it slipped in silently like a kid unsure if she belonged. Yet this expression succeeded in capturing the heart of child and youth. Indeed, it has come to be the most defining characteristic of what we call a Child and Youth Care approach (see chapter 2 of this book). Similar expressions have appeared from time to time, as others have expressed the idea that child and youth care involves, as Fritz Redl (1959) said, 'exploiting' the events that occur during the daily life of a child in care, for the benefit of that child (Fox, 1995). Redl's expression was not readily incorporated into the field, probably because of the political associations attached to the word 'exploiting'. Redl, of course, was talking about taking advantage of events, as they occur in the life space of the child. While the words may not have caught on, the idea certainly did. Just as the definition of child and youth care has come to include 'the relational' (Bellefeuille & Ricks, 2008; Garfat & Fulcher, 2012) and the meaning of 'life-space' has changed

1

(Gharabaghi & Stuart, 2013) so has the meaning of the phrase 'daily life events'. Whereas it used to refer primarily to what we might call the routines and rituals of everyday life (meals, bedtimes, etc.), it has come to refer to all the moments which occur in the life-space. This 'idea' has been evolving over time.

Maier (1987) encouraged us to attend to and use 'the minutiae' of everyday life, the little things, the small, seemingly unimportant events out of which the days of our lives are constructed: things like waiting for meal-times, occasions of leave-taking, or just simply coming into contact with one another. Followers of Redl suggest the use of life space interviews in which the care worker takes advantage of a singular event or moment (such as an argument between two youth) as it is occurring or immediately after it occurs, specifically entering into the immediate life of the child (Brendtro & Long, 2002). Peterson (1988) suggested watching for naturally occurring therapeutic opportunities that present themselves in the course of daily living. Guttmann (1991) suggested that care workers must enter into the flow of immediacies of the child's experiencing. In this way they can use interventions which are congruent with the flow of that experiencing (Fulcher, 1991). Entering into this flow of experiencing as it is occurring, and helping the child to live differently in the context within which they find themselves (Fewster, 1990), is central to impactful child and youth care practice. This focus on what we might call joint experiencing between child and worker, and the facilitation of the opportunity for change within this joint experiencing highlights the commonly identified CYC characteristic of 'doing with'. In many ways, it is what distinguishes our work from the interventive efforts of other professionals. In impactful child and youth care practice, the worker becomes, with the child, the co-creator of a therapeutic context (Durrant, 1993; Maier, 1994; Peterson, 1988) within which the child might experience the opportunity for change. This focus on the joint experiencing of what Garfat (2008) called the in-between between us is the essence of contemporary, relational Child and Youth Care Practice (Garfat & Fulcher, 2012) for it is through the everyday moments and opportunities that we might find the pathway to the creation of the truly relational experience. Recent

2

writings have demonstrated the use of daily life events in education, training, supervision, family work community and many other areas. Further, as Gharabaghi (2013) suggests, we are even finding ways to be present in the everyday moments of peoples' lives when we are not 'physically there'. Building on our powerful history, we are finding ways to make all moments meaningful.

Requirements

Child and youth care practice has evolved over time, and the expression 'the use of daily life events' might be rephrased as 'the entering into, and purposeful use of, daily life events, as they are occurring, for the benefit of the child, youth or family'. Such practice involves numerous skills, knowledge and ability on the part of child and youth care workers. They must, for example,

- have knowledge of child development (Maier, 1987),
- understand how to access and use that knowledge (Eisikovits, Beker, & Guttmann, 1991),
- know about the process of change (Garfat, Fulcher & Digney, 2019),
- possess an active self-awareness which allows the worker to distinguish self from other (Garfat, 1994; Ricks, 1989),
- be able to enter into an intimate caring relationship (Austin & Halpin, 1987, 1989) that involves attachment (Maier, 1993) and belonging (Brendtro, Brokenleg & Van Bockern, 2002),
- understand the process of meaning-making (Bruner, 1990; Krueger, 1994; VanderVen, 1992),
- have a framework for organizing their interventive actions (Eisikovits, Beker, & Guttmann, 1991; Garfat & Newcomen, 1992),
- understand the meaning and dynamics of relational practice (Garfat & Fulcher, 2012). understand how relationships create the life-space (Gharabaghi & Stuart, 2013),
- understand and be able to live the characteristics of Relational Child & Youth Care Practice (this book, Chapter 2)

3

All of this is necessary for recognising, using or even creating opportunities in the daily life events of a child, youth or family's life. The use of daily life events as they are occurring is one of the foundational characteristics that distinguish child and youth care practice from other forms of helping — which may also use daily life events, but at a distance removed from the immediacy of the experience itself.

The child and youth care focus on making everyday moments meaningful and therapeutic has been one of the most profound evolutions of our field and the more we focus on making moments meaningful in this way, the more helpful we will be to the young people and families with whom we work.

References

Austin, D., & Halpin, W (1987). Seeing "I to I": A phenomenological analysis of the caring relationship. *Journal of Child and Youth Care, 3*(3), 37-42.

Austin, D., & Halpin, W (1989). The caring response. *Journal of Child and Youth Care, 4*(3), 1-7.

Brendtro,L. K., Brokenleg, M. & Van Bockern, S. (2002). *Reclaiming youth at risk: Our hope for the future (2nd. ed.).* Bloomington, IL: Solution Tree.

Brendtro, L. K. & Long, N.J. (2002). *Controls from Within: The Enduring Challenge. Reclaiming Children and Youth* 11(1), Spring 2002, 5-9.

Bruner, J. *(1990). Acts of Meaning.* Cambridge, MA: Harvard University Press.

Durrant, M. (1993). *Residential treatment: A cooperative, competency-based approach to therapy and program design.* New York: WW Norton.

Eisikovits, Z., Beker, J., & Guttman, E. (1991). The known and the used in residential child and youth care work. In J. Beker & Z. Eisikovits (Eds.), *Knowledge utilization in residential child and youth care practice* (pp. 3-23). Washington, DC: Child Welfare League of America.

Fewster, G. (1990). *Being in child care: A journey into self.* New York: Haworth Press.

Fox, L. (1995). Exploiting daily events to heal the pain of sexual abuse. *Journal of Child and Youth Care,* 10(2), 33-42.

Fulcher, L. (1991). Teamwork in residential care. In J. Beker & Z. Eisikovits (Eds.), *Knowledge utilization in residential child and youth care practice* (pp. 2 15-235). Washington, DC: Child Welfare League of America.

Garfat, T. (1994). Never alone: Reflections on the presence of self and history on child and youth care. *Journal of Child and Youth Care Work,* 9(1), 35-43.

Garfat, T. (2008). The interpersonal in-between: An exploration of relational child and youth care practice. In G. Bellefuille & F. Ricks (Eds), pp 7-34. *Standing on the Precipice.* Edmonton: Macwen Press.

Garfat, T., Digney, J. & Fulcher. L.C. (2012). *The Therapeutic use of Daily Life Events (dle) training manual.*

Garfat, T. & Fulcher, L. (2012). *Child & Youth Care in Practice.* Cape Town: Pretext Publishing.

Garfat, T., & Newcomen, T. (1992). AS*IF: A model for child and youth care interventions. *Child and Youth Care Forum,* 21(4), 277-285.

Gharabaghi, K. (2013). Becoming present: The use of daily life events in family work. In T. Garfat, L.C. Fulcher & J. Digney (eds.), Making moments meaningful in child and youth care practice (pp.107-117). Cape Town: Pretext Publishing.

Gharabaghi, K. & Stuart, C. (2013). *Right here, right now: exploring life-space interventions for children and youth.* Toronto: Pearson.

Guttman, E. (1991). Immediacy in residential child and youth care work: The fusion of experience, self-consciousness, and action. In J. Beker & Z. Eisikovits (Eds.), *Knowledge utilization in residential child and youth care practice* (pp. 65-84). Washington, DC: Child Welfare League of America.

Krueger, M. (1994). Rhythm and presence: Connecting with children on the edge. *Journal of Emotional and Behavioral Problems,* 3(1), 49-51.

Maier, H.W (1987). *Developmental group care for children and youth: Concepts and practice.* New York: Haworth.

Maier, H.W (1993). Attachment development is "in". *Journal of Child and Youth Care,* 9(1), 35-52.

Maier, H.W (1994). A therapeutic environmental approach. *Research and Evaluation,* 3(2), 3-4

Peterson, R. (1988). The collaborative metaphor technique: Using Ericsonian (Milton H.) techniques and principles in child, family and youth care work. *Journal of Child Care,* 3(4), 11-27.

Redl, F. (1959). Strategy and technique of the Life-Space interview. *American Journal of Orthopsychiatry,* 29, 1-18.

Ricks, F. (1989). Self-awareness model for training and application in child and youth care. *Journal of Child and Youth Care,* 4(1), 33-42.

VanderVen, K. (1992). From the side of the swimming pool and the evolving story of child and youth care work. *Journal of Child and Youth Care Work,* 8, 5-6.

2

Characteristics of a Relational Child and Youth Care Approach (Revisited)

Thom Garfat, James Freeman, Kiaras Gharabaghi and Leon Fulcher

Introduction

A Brief History of the Characteristics

In 2004, Garfat (2004a) identified characteristics, drawn from research, classic and contemporary literature and his and others' experience of the field, which were thought to identify a Child and Youth Care (CYC) approach to caring. These characteristics were updated by Fulcher and Garfat (2008) when writing about their applicability in foster care and then again in a review of applications of a relational Child and Youth Care approach in a special issue of the *Relational Child and Youth Care Practice* journal (2011). These applications were further developed in *Making Moments Meaningful in CYC Practice* (Garfat, Fulcher & Digney, 2013), in *Child and Youth Care in Practice* (Garfat & Fulcher, 2012), and in *Child and Youth Care Practice with Families* (Fulcher & Garfat, 2015). Subsequent writings expressed how the characteristics were applicable to specific practices of supervision (Charles, Freeman & Garfat, 2016) and trauma responsive care (Freeman, 2015a). These characteristics are again updated and presented here based on readings, workshops, conferences, discussions and insights drawn from the field in the past few years.

About this Revision

This updated version of the 25 characteristics represents a significant enhancement from previous versions. It acknowledges and includes many significant voices that are important to the field. It also acknowledges that the field of Child and Youth Care has, over a period of decades, been complacent in its approach to centering the lived experiences of Indigenous, racialized, non-binary gendered, neuro-diverse bodies, presenting instead a list of characteristics that can be read as fundamentally 'white', ablelist, and heteronormative (Gharabaghi, 2016; Vachon, 2018, Skott-Myhre, 2017). We have also learned a lot about the effects of trauma on young people, including generational trauma as well as abuse and neglect.

This new version of the 25 characteristics is not a critique of previous versions; it is instead a way of re-contextualizing the characteristics within lived experiences and intersectionalities in an effort to provide a foundation (albeit one in need of constant growth and adaptation) for Child and Youth Care practice moving forward. Collectively, we set out to reimagine the 25 characteristics by engaging over 100 Child and Youth Care involved people (broadly defined) from North America and the Caribbean, Africa, Asia, Australia and Europe in order to open dialogue among differently located and positioned individuals to reflect on the characteristics and provide suggestions for rendering these commensurate with the many different ways people are connected to the field. Through this process, the 25 characteristics were reviewed by individuals with longstanding involvement in the field and its community, as well as by many individuals thinking and writing from perspectives and with identities reflecting various contexts including trauma, multiple racial, gender, ability/disability, sexual orientation, and class positions.

In reflecting on the feedback we received, we must first express how grateful we are that so many individuals provided detailed, serious, meaningful suggestions for shifting the nuances and the scope of the 25 characteristics to such an inclusive and relevant space. We are especially grateful for the feedback from individuals who have long encountered barriers, sometimes invisible to us, in attempting to access this field and the community that comes with it. We are equally grateful for the expression of relevance and meaning that these characteristics have in such diverse geographies, experiences and cultural spaces. We heard about how these characteristics have been helpful in Isibindi projects in South Africa, in residential settings across Canada, in post-secondary education settings in Europe, North America and Africa, and in community-based child and youth care services in Australia and Asia. We learned that the field, broadly defined, is fundamentally interested in continuing discussions and exploration of the following themes:

- The role of power embedded in racist ideologies, state and institutional structures, and cultural hegemonies;

- A critical perspective on the universality of core concepts, including care, love and relational practice;

- The importance of historical events and practices and their connection to generational and on-going trauma;

- Acknowledging, especially in Canada, the United States and Australia, Indigenous ways of knowing, experiencing, and sharing;

- Framing Child and Youth Care practice as an approach rather than a rigidly defined professional practice with impenetrable borders for individuals and groups of people with different lived experiences based on race, gender, ability/disability and other criteria.

We also learned about, and are pleased to express our commitment to, the need for on-going reflection on, and revision of, these 25 characteristics, always with the voices of diverse individuals and groups as partners. In many respects, we (the authors) do not own these characteristics. They belong to our diverse field and the people who are drawing on these characteristics as a way of being in the world.

Defining a Relational Child and Youth Care Approach

We believe that Child and Youth Care practitioners are ideally situated to be among the most influential of healers and helpers in a person or family's life. For many years, the work that Child and Youth Care practitioners do was considered, at best, a sub-profession and the workers themselves were frequently considered to be extensions of other helping professionals, most commonly Social Workers (Garfat & Charles, 2010). However, with the passage of time and the evolution of a distinct approach to practice, Child and Youth Care (CYC)[1] and CYC practitioners, like social pedagogues in Europe and child care workers in South Africa, have come to be recognized as possessing a specific expertise and a unique approach to working with children, youth and families (Fulcher & Garfat, 2015; Mann-Feder, Scott, & Hardy, 2017; Thumbadoo, 2008) involving a "comprehensive framework for being with young people in relational and authentic ways" (Gharabaghi, 2017a, p. 5).

A CYC practitioner's position in the daily life of another person, and/or their family and community, allows the practitioner to intervene proactively, responsively and immediately to assist others to develop different ways of acting and experiencing in the world (Fulcher & Garfat, 2008). There is no other form of helping which is so immediate, so grounded in the present experiencing or, one might say, so everyday. This immediacy of being present as helpers creates in-the-moment learning opportunities (Ward, 1998) allowing the individual to experiment with alternative ways of acting and experiencing as they are living their lives. CYC practice is not oriented around temporally spaced and infrequent visits to an

---

1   The term Child and Youth Care (CYC) is used here in both the specific and generic sense. While it does refer to those practitioners in a variety of countries who carry the title of CYC worker, it also refers to those who might practice within a Child and Youth Care framework but be identified with different titles such as youth worker, social pedagogue, residential social worker, and across multiple settings.

9

office where the 'client' meets with a therapist who has little to no experience of the individual's experiences in everyday life. Rather, it is based on being in-the-moment with the individual(s), experiencing their life and living with it them as it unfolds (Baizerman, 1999; Winfield, 2008), within an inclusive, rights-based, anti-oppressive and trauma-informed framework that extends from the nature of inter-personal relations to the engagement of systemic and institutional features of injustice (Daniel, 2016). Child and youth care practice seeks to avoid the pitfalls of being with others as framed eloquently by Hooks (2000): "When we face pain in relationships, our first response is to sever bonds rather than to maintain commitment." We remember, always, that young people are the authors of their own story (history) and, ultimately, the agents of their own change (Gharabaghi & Stuart, 2011).

Child and Youth Care practice is based on helping people think about and live their life differently, as they are living it (Freeman, 2015b; Garfat, 2002). It is a focused, timely, practical and, above all, immediately responsive form of caring which uses "applied learning and daily uses of knowledge to inform more responsive daily encounters with children or young people" (Fulcher 2004, p. 34). It is immediate and focused on the moment as it is occurring. It allows for the individual to learn, experience and practice different thoughts, feelings and actions in the most important area of their lives – daily life as they are living it (Gannon, 2014; Mucina, 2012).

We recognize that becoming involved in a person's or family's life is more than an inter-personal process; it requires an engagement with the context of history and its consequences, including, for example, the histories of residential schools and deeply embedded biases impacting Indigenous communities across North America, as well as anti-Black racism, gender normativity, sexual conservatism, neuro-diversity and other histories of oppression and racism around the world. Still we believe that Child and Youth Care practitioners are ideally situated to impact the circumstances of young people, their families and their communities precisely because CYC practice offers a unique way of being in the world, and therefore of being with young people, their families, and their communities in the context of their present situation.

The Characteristics as a Framework for Practice

The diagram below (Freeman & Garfat, 2014) shows how these characteristics of a Child and Youth Care approach are arranged around the purposeful use of daily life events and grouped according to processes of Being, Interpreting and Doing (Freeman & Garfat, 2014). These characteristics are foundational to our way of being, interpreting and doing in our work, wherever our work is located. They characterize the Child and Youth Care way of being in the world with other(s).

This approach outlined by these characteristics aims for inclusiveness, an equitable joining together of all who participate in the field. Thus, one might be, for example, a Child and Youth Care worker, a CYC instructor, a family worker, a trainer, a youth advocate, a community development worker, a researcher, a supervisor, etc. What binds them together, as CYC practitioners, is the shared approach to their work. Thus, CYC practitioners are connected by how they think about and carry out their work. Child and Youth Care is, after all, an 'approach' or a way of being in the world with others. So, we aim here to be inclusive while acknowledging the historic context of trauma, power, and 'privilege and cultural singularity' (Gharabaghi, 2017b) which is the history of our field. Indeed, as Skott-Myhre said, all of us "need to seek to be accountable to our privilege in real and material ways" (2017, p. 17) and recognize the political aspects of our work.

The 25 characteristics of relational Child and Youth Care Practice are not intended to capture, for example, the limiting world of institutional care and traditional designations within the professional field of Child and Youth Care. They are, quite to the contrary, meant to reflect a particular approach to 'being with', whether this is framed around euro-centric ideas of developmental growth or, for example, Indigenous ideas about the 'Healing Path' (McCabe, 2007). Ultimately, the Characteristics are about child and youth care practice in the life-space and in the moment. They do not represent an analysis of social systems, institutions or processes. They make no attempt to comprehensively capture the richness of literature that speaks to anti-oppressive practices, marginalization, system change and advocacy. And they are certainly not meant to provide a foundation for policy frameworks. The characteristics speak to how we are with young people, in all of their diversity and life experiences, understanding that people's lives are very much impacted by social structures, power relations, racism, exclusion, marginalization and other dynamics.

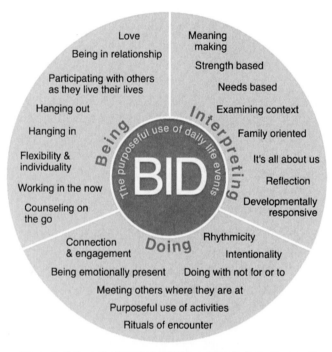

Characteristics of a Relational Child and Youth Care Approach

Freeman, J. & Garfat, T. (2014). Being, interpreting, doing: A framework for organizing the characteristics of a relational child and youth care approach. *Child & Youth Care Online, 179,* 23-27. Retrieved from http://www.cyc-net.org/cyc-online/jan2014.pdf

Relational Child and Youth Care Practice

Relational Child and Youth Care practice is an approach in which attention is directed towards 'the in-between between us' (Garfat, 2008). As Bellefeuille and Jamieson noted "relational practice is a dynamic, rich, flexible, and continually evolving process of co-constructed inquiry. In this type of inquiry, meaning emerges within the 'space between' the individual, family, or community" (2008, p. 38). The co-constructed nature of the in-between is a central feature of effective relational Child and Youth Care practice. Without a focus on the in-between between us, there is no relational practice.

This co-created space, *the in-between between us*, represents the 'hub of the wheel' around which all characteristics of Child and Youth Care practice revolve. We often call this co-created space between us the relationship, but relational practice involves much more than just 'having a relationship' (whether good or not) with another person. Rather, it means that the practitioner is constantly attending to the co-created space between self and other, wondering, for example, 'Is it a safe enough place?"; 'Is it a learning space?'; 'Is it a developmentally appropriate place of experience?'; 'Is it a place of pain? Of joy?'; 'Of inclusion and equity?'. The practitioner also continuously reflects on the nature of power embedded within this co-created space, recognizing the inherent power imbalance between practitioner and young person that can be further accentuated through racial, gender and other expressions of individuality. Honouring the space between Self and other includes an active, present and transparent acknowledgment of power. The focus, however, is more on the characteristics of the co-created relationship itself, than on those of the individuals in the relationship. As Gharabaghi (2014, p. 8) explained 'relational practice shifts the focus from the actors engaged in some form of interaction to the experience of interacting regardless of the specific actors'. A focus on the in-between between us, concentrates on the experience itself with an understanding that this experience is subject to, or even mediated by, externally situated and historically burdened structures, institutions, and processes which involved generational trauma, racial, cultural, and material power dynamics.

The creation of this in-between space is impacted by the self-identity, culture, historical context and practice setting of those involved in this co-creating (Gharabaghi, 2014). How do, for example, the current contexts and cultural histories of a middle-aged Polish male immigrant CYC and an indigenous Cree female teenager from Northern Canada, intersect to impact on the evolution of their relational space in the context of a large city drop-in shelter? It becomes complex indeed.

A focus on the 'in-between between us' ensures that the Child and Youth Care practitioner remains attentive to the mutuality of relationship, recognizing that both parties to the relationship create and are influenced by it (Fewster, 1990, 2001). We are all impacted by our encounter in the in-between. Stuart argued that "the relationship *is* the intervention" (2009, p. 222) and a focus on the relational aspects of practice, as described here, helps to ensure that the CYC practitioner maintains this focus on the relational in-between. The understanding of the multiple identity dimensions both parties bring to that in-between space and the ways in which those identities can simultaneously intersect and compete, is central to how the relational dynamic unfolds.

As Fewster said, relational practice "is not only a very different perspective; it is a different pathway, across a very different terrain, in search of a very different destination". (Fewster, 2005a, p. 3). It is, as Krueger (2004, n.p.) pointed out "a way of being with youth in the lived experience" in which both parties must experience *relational safety* (Garfat, 2016) requiring an inclusive focus on what each bring to the evolution of the relational space. It is a focus on 'how you are, who you are, while you do what you do' (Garfat, 2013). Relational practice is a way of being in the world with others in which the focus is on connectedness, not individuation (Fletcher, 1998) or isolation while recognizing that each individual's experiences can impact on how they are in the world and how they see themselves positioned in the world.

In the following, 25 characteristics of a Relational Child and Youth Care approach are identified, high-lighted and organised according to a framework we call BID – Being, Interpreting and Doing – which represents an effective foundation for describing the Child and Youth Care process of connecting to promote growth, change and learning (see, for example, Bristow, 2017; Freeman & Garfat, 2014). The BID sections should not be considered as sequential or linear but rather as inherently connected. For example, while I am Doing, I am also still Interpreting and Being. While at times there may be a greater focus on one element of this triad, the practitioner is Being, Interpreting and Doing at all times. The characteristics are conceptualized around the idea of the 'purposeful use of daily life events' which we see as central to, and the defining characteristic of, effective relational Child and Youth Care practice. Each of the other characteristics

"demonstrate how this use of daily life events integrates into the larger CYC approach as well as describe the qualities of those who use daily live events effectively. The use of daily life events links to each of the other characteristics and unifies them in a structured system" (Freeman & Garfat, 2014, 23-27).

Characteristics of a Relational Child and Youth Care Approach

The characteristics and descriptions which follow evolved through discussions, observations, readings, dialogues and other encounters with the field of Child and Youth Care practice, with a focus on the relational. They do not completely reflect, perhaps, how we would 'like' CYC practice to be. Rather they reflect a collective observation of aspects of the field as identified at the time of this writing. Thus, these characteristics represent an inherent tension, in as much as the field *as it is* has often limited itself to very particular mechanisms of inclusion that have inadvertently excluded many lived experiences based on race, gender identity, sexuality, disability and others. The characteristics nevertheless seek to take account of ways of being, ways of interpreting, and ways of doing that seek to be inclusive of lived experiences. We recognise that the field is evolving constantly and expect that these characteristics will become even more defined and expansive in the future.

The characteristics have been organised into three (3) groupings: Being, Interpreting and Doing. This framework (BIDs) evolved from the work of practitioners (Freeman & Garfat, 2014) as a way of thinking about the process of intervention within the field of Child and Youth Care practice. But we are also aware that while we are making bids for connection so, too, young people, when they are able to, make bids to connect with us. While young people sometimes cannot or are not able to make such bids for connection, we are constantly on the alert to notice them, however they might occur.

> "Together the three categories – Being, Interpreting, and Doing – form the acronym BID, highlighting the bids for connection that are at the center of our relational work. To make a bid is the act of making an offer for something. It is an old word dating from before the twelfth century and is defined as an "attempt or effort to win, achieve, or attract" (Merriam-Webster, n.d.) as in making a bid for reelection" (Freeman & Garfat, 2014, 25).

This framework for organisation highlights anchor characteristics in each of the three areas.

> "The anchor characteristics provide strength and support to the other characteristics within each category. Identifying anchors within each category offers practical guidance to those beginning in the field as they focus on their own development. It prioritizes, in a way, what might be an essential starting point in one's personal growth and development. The three anchors in this framework include:
>
> Love – in the category of Being
> Meaning making – in the category of Interpreting
> Connection & engagement – in the category of Doing."

(Freeman and Garfat, 2014, p. 26)

The following describes and articulates the 25 characteristics and their relevance in relational Child and Youth Care practice in today's world.

Being

> "Being in relationship means that we have what it takes to remain open and responsive in conditions where most mortals – and

professionals – quickly distance themselves, become 'objective' and look for the external 'fix.'" (Fewster, 2004)

Love serves as a "prerequisite of healthy development" (Smith, 2011) and a lack of a basic love for others and a willingness to be stretched and grow in that love may be an indication of the need for an individual to consider a different field. (Freeman & Garfat, 2014, p. 26).

Love is inclusive – regardless of who, or how, you are, you belong in this endeavor – if you are connected at all, you are a part of it. Extended family, community and community members, people of cultures different than the practitioner, multiple support staff, intimate friends, etc. – all are a part of this process of engaging in an appropriate response to the young person and family, based on this foundation of love. To be inclusive means to accept people for who and how they are while acknowledging that everyone brings to the relational encounter their own history and that history requires recognition, understanding, valuing and acceptance if we are to focus on the creation of relational safety (Garfat, 2016). It means "honoring differences and accepting diversity as a norm" (InclusionBC, 2018).

Inclusiveness also implies that while I invite other(s) to be a part of my experience (process) I also work to create the experiences where they will include me in theirs. Inclusiveness is a goal, often illusive and always significant. It requires that I, as an individual, attend to what helps the other person(s) feel included – how do they prefer to be identified, what is important to them, what would count as an inclusive gesture? I also must attend to how they need me to be in order to want to include me in their world of experience for, if inclusiveness is seen as a one-way street where I am the one 'including other', and not worried about them including me, then it is not a relationship based on equity (Marshall, 2017). So, one is constantly wondering 'how do I need to be or what do I need to do in order for this person to experience inclusion?' What effort am I applying to this end? The 'what I have to do?' may focus on my interaction and may also include 'how to I need to act on our environmental context so that it expresses and invites inclusion?' The practitioner recognizes that it may not be possible to be or to become what the young person needs. I cannot be Indigenous or Black or Transgendered if in fact I am white and cis-gendered. But the practitioner can extend the invitation to being with and doing with the young person even in the context of limitations presented by fixed identities. Inclusion is an interactive and an environmental consideration.

Love, as Thumbadoo (2011) writing from a South African context argued, is present in powerful Child and Youth Care moments with (an) other. She asserts that love must be present when real connections are made between self and other. This is not, of course, a sexual love but a love of (an) other as a human being in the Ubuntu sense of "I am because you are". Thumbadoo (2011, p. 197) further asserts that "caring and love intermingle in the encounters" between CYC practitioners and others". While Thumbadoo writes from the South African context, her words are echoed elsewhere. Mark Smith (2011, p. 192), writing from a United Kingdom context, claims that "child and youth care – in contrast perhaps to other professions or aspiring professions – is irredeemably a practical, moral and relational endeavor. As such, it is fertile ground for the growth of love". Whitfield has said that "love is the most healing of our resources" (1989, p. 133). Relational CYC practice is, in this sense, an act of love and loving – one holds others dear, one cherishes their being, and ultimately one acts in the context of love in a non-exploitative manner, accepting and honouring other for who and how they are. As Ranahan (2000, p. 57) said, when discussing love in CYC practice, "a more mature form of love, can exist in practice when we choose to include it, even in a brief moment of our connectedness with a child". An edition of the Scottish Journal of Residential Child Care (2017) has also affirmed the importance, and role, of love in our field.

Being in relationship is not the same as 'having a relationship'. Everyone *has* relationships but *'being in relationship'* means engaging with the other person in an intimate and profound manner which impacts both young person *and* helper (Gannon, 2008). A

CYC practitioner recognizes that they engage in a relationship with a person where each has contributed to making that relationship what it is (Fewster, 1990), even when the young person may have first encountered the practitioner under the circumstances of someone else's choosing (such as an involuntary residential placement). It also means engaging in relationships and being in these relationships with intention for whatever time is available.

While being-in-relationship might well be a universal characteristic of relational CYC practice, *how* one engages in relationship and the meaning of such engagement will be influenced by the history, culture, identity, capabilities and other aspects of the participants to this co-creation of the in-between. Thus, when we make efforts to be-in-relationship with other we are constantly contextualizing our actions and understanding in terms of the attributes we each bring to this encounter. As we shall see when considering the characteristic of Meaning-Making, what counts as an inviting gesture to one person may be experienced quite differently by the other – constant reflection, therefore, permeates our attempts to work towards being-in-relationship with other(s).

Relationships are comprised of a history and that history continues to shape the relationship and our being in such relationships. Writing about UK social work practices with young people in care, Thomas came to similar conclusions about the importance children give to relationships including "the continuity of this relationship, reliability and availability, confidentiality, advocacy and doing things together" (2005, p. 189). As Fewster said, "Being in relationship means that we have what it takes to remain open and responsive in conditions where most mortals – and professionals – quickly distance themselves, become 'objective' and look for the external fix" (2004, p. 3). Being in relationship, then, means that you and I encounter and *be* with one another in the in-between between us (Garfat, 2008). Being in relationship requires that we are constantly reflecting on the intersectionalities of self and other(s).

Being and participating with people in the everyday moments of their lives*.* Whether it is with a family in their home as they are doing dishes or playing soccer with a young person in the

19

community park; attending a human rights rally with a person concerned about their community, or chatting with a homeless youth on the streets; whether it involves hanging out with a mother in jail, engaging an autistic student, or participating with a young person in a church activity – CYC practitioners involve themselves in all aspects of the daily life of the people with whom they work (Fulcher & Ainsworth, 2006; Hilton, 2002; Smart, 2006). As Bristow (2017, p. 19) said, when talking about working with people with autism, being with people "as they live their lives can be as simple as checking in throughout the day, or it can involve a more thorough involvement in their lives". Young people author their own narratives, their own stories that capture their experience of life (Gharabaghi & Stuart (2011) and the role of the CYC practitioner is to become a significant character in their stories wherever those stories unfold.

When a CYC educator, for example, encounters a student in the cafeteria, the CYC responds to the student from a CYC perspective. When a CYC practitioner on the street encounters a young person, that worker remembers to interact using the characteristics of a relational CYC approach. The worker attends, for example, to a young person's relationships with the other inhabitants of their street life, their identity and the socio-cultural context that frames their identity. Central to a CYC approach is the idea that if people can change how they are (develop different or new ways of being and / or doing), in the minutia of their lives (Maier, 1979), then change will be more enduring, for their relationships are central to who they are and how they are in their world and the world of others. Being and participating with people as they live their life, where they live their lives, increases the potential for them to develop new ways of being in their everyday world. And we remember, always, that sometimes the necessary changes are not in how the young people are, but, rather, changes are needed in the world which surrounds them.

Partnering with young people to challenge the world as it is and as it impacts them in particular, is one core element of being with young people as they live their lives. For Indigenous young people, for example, living their lives means also living deeply embedded racism, many symptoms of exclusion and few opportunities to live the spirit of their cultures, their languages or their rituals. Practitioners recognize that in today's world, enduring change requires enduring advocacy through committed partnership with young people, their families and their communities.

Hanging out means that some of the CYC practitioner's time is spent doing apparently simple, everyday (yet extremely important) things with people (Garfat, 1999). To an outsider, it may seem as though nothing is happening. A walk in the park or ritualistically sipping tea with a family; kicking stones with a young person; browsing through cyber-space, chatting in the corridor, wheeling someone along the street, or leaning on a street lamp chatting with a homeless young person – all may seem like 'doing nothing' when, in fact, these may be the most important of activities. During such moments and experiences of 'hanging out' one is investing in building relationships of trust, safety, connectedness, and professional intimacy. In this *hanging out* control and power are set aside by the CYC as much as possible; rather, it is more an encounter, simply, of people hanging out together hopefully in the context of the young person's life space. And this takes time – something often missed as finance controllers scan quickly through monthly and yearly accounts or supervisors review a 'shift report' of notable incidences. These are the very types of relationships which are necessary if the practitioner is to become a significant and influential person included in the life of others (House of Commons Select Committee, 2009; Redl, 1952).

Hanging In means that the Child and Youth Care practitioner does not give up when 'times are tough', even if, as hooks (2000) pointed out, this may be the intuitive response. Rather, one hangs in and works things through, demonstrating commitment and caring for that child, young person or parents and family members (Gompf, 2003). The traumatized child or young person in a foster home who is struggling to follow expectations, the Indigenous youth struggling to re-connect with cultural traditions, the Syrian student who is struggling to grasp a North American custom, the parent from another country who struggles with learning to parent according to 'expectations and demands' of a new culture, the research subjects who find it difficult to appear for interviews, or the person with a 'disability' trying to be in the world with others unable to see beyond the 'disability' and, therefore, do not engage with the full person – for CYC Practitioners these are all signs of the need to hang in. Sometimes things are 'tough' for the young person, sometimes for the practitioner and sometimes for both but hanging in means not giving up.

It requires that one be patient and move at the other's pace rather than the practitioner's own pace (Fulcher, 2006b) or the expectation of the program or service model. As a practitioner, for example, reaches out to connect with someone who has a history and context which warns against immediate connection, the practitioner also needs to hang in and not become frustrated while exploring new or culturally different ways of making that connection.

Equally, when times seem 'good', the practitioner does not automatically assume that 'all is well'. Steckley and Kendrick (2008) highlighted implications associated with *'holding on' while 'hanging in'*; signaling the importance trauma sensitive forms of physical restraint as extreme examples of this characteristic. One must recognize that when the times are good, set-backs may be just around the corner. After all, learning and change, indeed healing, take time effort, practice, and learning from feedback.

Working in the now means that the Child and Youth Care practitioner remains focused on the 'here and now', on what is happening in this moment between the practitioner and the other person (Freeman, 2014; Phelan, 2009). This allows the practitioner the opportunity to enhance their ability to "recognize and respond to behaviors as they are occurring" (Freeman, 2014, p. 14). Such an orientation on the present arises from the assumption that 'we are who we are, wherever we are' and that we bring our whole selves to every interaction. At the same time, this orientation to the here and now does not negate our continuous awareness of structural and systemic contexts that may contribute to individuals or families engaging in behaviours as reasonable and necessary defense mechanisms against racism, generational trauma. marginalization, exclusion and oppression.

In the present, one carries with them the past as well as expectations about the future (Winfield, 2005). If a person can change their way of being with another or other(s) in the present, so too can they generalize that way of being to other situations in their life. Past experiences can become even more important learning cues in the here and now. Similarly, expectations about the future or future consequences can also change through new lived experiences in daily life events as they happen.

Counseling on the go. Unlike in other forms of helping, a Child and Youth Care practitioner does not normally meet with someone for a counseling session at a scheduled time and place (although that occasionally does happen and can be valuable). The counseling which occurs between a CYC practitioner and the other(s) typically occurs through fragmented but connected interactions, trusting that the ability of the other and the skill of the CYC practitioner will continue to connect such moments together into a coherent process (Krueger, 1999). Some refer to this CYC characteristic as 'life-space counseling' (Redl & Wineman, 1952). Here we notice the important role in which each relationship history impacts on present and future prospects for facilitated learning. As Mann-Feder (2011) explains, these moments of connected interaction are often more powerful than traditional approaches to 'talk therapy' precisely because they happen in moments of movement and activity when motivation to learn and try new things is high and relevant.

Flexibility and individuality refer to the fact that every person and family is unique. Each person brings to the relational encounter a history of previous life experiences which may include relationships of pain, a history of oppression, positive encounters with adults, feelings of worthiness or unworthiness, experiences of racism, and the list could go on forever. What is important is that the practitioner recognizes that all these previous experiences are an important part of the context of the encounter and are a part of what influences, self or other, the person in their present context. Even historic trauma, racism, or abuse accumulates and can impact the present moment for an individual or family. The effective CYC practitioner is aware of this dynamic and adjusts their approach respectfully.

All of one's interventions must be tailored to fit the person and/or family as the practitioner understands them (Michael, 2005) and has learned about, and from, them. This means that the CYC practitioner is flexible in their interactions with each person, recognizing that there is no one approach or intervention which fits for everyone, or applies in all situations. Just because the last time the practitioner intervened in a particular manner when engaging with a person from a culture different than the practitioner's, and that action was successful, does not mean that all people from that culture will respond in the same manner. All people, in their unique cultural context, are different and individual. Just because one young person liked a joke when they were in pain, this does not mean that another young person will respond likewise (Digney, 2007). As deFinney, Loiselle and Dean (2010, p. 72) said, we always must take account of "the intersecting effects of gender, race, sexuality, (dis)ability, and age formations, among others". Just as CYC practitioners are individuals, so it is for everyone with whom they work. Thus, CYC practitioners must be ever flexible, preparing to modify their approach and way of being as appropriate with each unique individual they encounter. From this flows the contemporary reflection that 'one size does not fit all' (Naidoo, 2005) and any intervention must be considered in the light of both individuals specific history and current identity. This identified way of being with others is a unique contribution which CYC practitioners bring in supporting children, youth and families in today's world.

Interpreting

Meaning making is the process through which each of us – worker or child – interprets everything else including, for example, what constitutes a strength of character. (Freeman, 2013).

Meaning-Making refers to the process a person goes through in making sense of their experiences (Garfat, 2004b; Steckley & Smart, 2005). An action occurs – one interprets it according to their own way of making sense of things – and then acts according to that perception. The other person in any interaction does exactly the same. Thus, two people may respond very differently to a simple gesture because of what it means to them. What is important is not 'what one meant to say or do' but how the practitioner's words or actions are interpreted by the other person. Saying hello, for example, to one young person on the streets may be interpreted as a gesture of inclusion, while to another it may signal betrayal. A male offering to shake hands with a woman of one culture may be interpreted as a gesture of equality, while to a woman from another culture it may signal invasion and disrespect. Things mean what they mean to the individual. Most of us behave in a manner which suggests that 'our way' of seeing the world is 'the right way' of seeing the world, and this is just not true. The CYC practitioner must guard against this unfortunate human tendency.

The process of meaning-making is influenced by many factors and just as the practitioner must be concerned about what influences the young person's process of meaning making, so must the practitioner reflect equally on their own. How, for example, might a white middle class Canadian male, be influenced in the process of making meaning by a history of privilege or upbringing in the cultural context of a white euro-centric family history which includes the colonial history of perceiving self as the savior or hero 'protecting and saving' others? As Brokenleg said: "Our worldviews are shaped by our cultural and family attachments. Each of us drags around our cultural tail, a thousand years long as well as our more personal family tale (1998, p. 139) and "the way we and others see the world and make meaning in part is determined by the rituals, traditions, views and beliefs of our culture and families" (Krueger, 2006). Meaning making is central and inherent in every interaction we have with another person.

Examining Context requires one to be conscious of how everything that occurs does so in a context unique to the helper, the other, the specific moment of interaction and the history of such interactions (Krueger & Stuart, 1999). Some elements of context may be the same such as national and regional policies, political environment, agency philosophy, regulations, or the physical environment. Even when elements of context are the same, however, how these are experienced may differ substantially, especially when elements such as racism, exclusion or marginalization are considered. Other elements of context (e.g., cultural traditions, trauma histories, personal experiences of being cared for, previous relationships with adults, developmental stage, specific capabilities) vary with the individual interactions between CYC practitioner and the other person (Fulcher, 2006a). The interaction, for example, between a university student and a CYC instructor is contextualized by the meaning of education to both participants, the power in the relationship between the two as well as the power dynamics perpetuated by the institution as a symbol of dominant classes, racial, gender and other hegemonies. The structures and expectations of the university, the philosophies about education and many more things impact on the moment of interaction. Thus, no two contexts can ever be the same and the CYC practitioner is constantly examining all these elements so as to understand and engage with the moment more fully. Relational practice which does not include an awareness of the specific context of the multi-layered, lived experiences of others is insufficient (Munroe, 2017) for effective CYC practice.

A Needs-Based Focus assumes that everything one does, is done for a purpose (Hill, 2001). That purpose is to meet personal or social needs, although one cannot assume that everyone is constantly aware of what need they are trying to meet. As CYC practitioners, the task is to help people identify their needs and to find more satisfying ways of meeting them. When one helps a person to find a different, more satisfying, way of meeting a need then the previous way of meeting the need (usually an undesirable behaviour) is no longer necessary (Maier, 1979). Thus, it becomes easier for that person to let go of such behaviour. The young person who belongs to a gang may be meeting the need for belonging. A partner having an affair may be meeting the need to feel valued. A young runaway may be meeting a need for safety. The student who 'acts out' in class may be meeting a need to be noticed by others.

While there are many frameworks which purport to identify human needs, a needs-based focus addresses human needs with direct and clear language (e.g., a need to be noticed or cared for, a need to matter to someone, experience connection or safety). Existing models of basic needs inform rather than limit such application.

Strengths-Based. The Child and Youth Care practitioner is positioned to seek out the strengths of the other(s) in whatever context they are encountered. It is, in fact, a primary task of CYC practitioners (Freeman, 2013). The practitioner admires, for example, the resilience of street youths and their ability to survive in a dangerous world. The practitioner identifies strengths in families who think all is lost and appreciates and rejoices in a student's determination to master a difficult concept or the autistic child's efforts to communicate. This focus on strengths and resilience enables others to also experience themselves as competent and worthy (Brendtro & Larson, 2005). Quite often this may represent the beginnings of a new experience of self for many of the children and young people with whom CYC practitioners work. Gilligan (2009) claimed that resilience is about doing well in adversity. As CYC practitioners reframe their thinking towards a strengths-based orientation, not only do they support the resilience of the children and young people with whom they work, they are also empowered themselves.

Developmentally Responsive Practice means that the Child and Youth Care practitioner attends to the relevant developmental characteristics of each individual (Fulcher & Garfat, 2008; Maier, 1987). Rather than simply reacting to their behaviour, the practitioner responds to the person's needs in a manner which is proactively consistent with their developmental stage and needs (Small & Fulcher, 2006). Here one considers development not from a chronological perspective but rather from a capacity perspective.

This enables the practitioner to consider each person as an individual with strengths and challenges in different areas since nobody develops consistently across all areas of their potential. When thinking of families, the practitioner also considers their developmental stage and potential, recognizing that not all families develop according to some predetermined plan and that the concept of development commonly differs across cultures. In fact, quite differently than in traditional developmental psychology, the CYC developmental perspective is focused on confidence building around the demonstrated capacities of the young person or a family or even a community in order to aspire to further accomplishments. In this way, the CYC practitioner can operate from within a framework of neuro-diversity, and the many different ways in which developmental process is articulated and critiqued across traumatized, racialized and gendered communities.

It's All about Us refers to the fact that, ultimately, interactions with other people are profoundly influenced by who CYC practitioners are themselves, As Burford and Fulcher noted there is "an important interplay between the diagnostic characteristics of residents and the patterns of staff team functioning found in any residential group care centre" (2006, p. 202-203). It is only through a deep and active self-awareness that the practitioner can be reassured that their actions are in the interest of the other(s) and not simply the CYC practitioner meeting their own needs, or that working over any length of time with particular young people may impact directly on a practitioner's actual state of being (Mattingly, 2006). 'It's all about us' also refers to the fact that one is not operating alone. The plural pronoun 'us' refers to everyone involved in helping another person grow and develop. This holds for all CYC practitioners, whether their titles be Foster Carer, Kinship Carer, Birth Family member, Young Person, Social Worker, Teacher, Therapist, Manager, Play Group or Youth Group leader, Peer Mentor, Distant Relatives, Clan or Tribal members, etc., Each has a role to play. The more everyone is working together, unified and not 'us and them', the more successful everyone will be in supporting developmental outcomes for the people with whom we work.

Abraham (2009) refers to this as 'Team Parenting'. Milligan and Stevens (2006) spoke about this as collaborative practice. It is thus argued that the CYC approach is holistic, ecological and inclusive. Ultimately, "We're all in this together!"

Family-Oriented. There was a time when family was not considered to be an important part of the Child and Youth Care field. Indeed, CYC workers were often encouraged to think of family as 'the enemy' – the cause of the problems of the child or young person with whom they were working (Shaw & Garfat, 2004). Now CYC practitioners recognize that family is important (Ainsworth, 2006). Families – including extended family members, clan or tribe – are ever present. The student in the classroom carries the expectations of family and extended family members. The young person on the street carries 'family' – even if only the ideal family – in their head. Many youths also choose their family, selecting those who are meaningful to them. Families with whom CYC practitioners work are not only present but so, too, are the families and extended families of the parents. Families may exist or be imagined in local geographies (and therefore be physically accessible) or in distant and even transnational spaces, with many intersections of language, family rituals and traditions, and social values. Also present are the family and extended families of the CYC practitioner, whether working the floor, or engaging in supervision. The competent practitioner is ever mindful that there is no such thing, really, as helping in the absence of family and extended family members. This is because family – in whatever form or tradition – is always with us and also with each person the CYC practitioner encounters (Garfat & Charles, 2010) and that 'family' is best identified by whom the young person identifies as family, not by the traditional cultural norms.

Reflection is the process one goes through when thinking about one's work: What have we done? What are we doing here? What might we do in the future? How is my history impacting on the current situation? How have traumatic experiences in the past impacted this current interaction? What biases am I holding, consciously or unconsciously, which may be of importance here? How is the power I hold (e.g., as a result of my professional position, privilege, economic means, gender identity, abilities) impacting the current circumstance and how is the power of the space I am in impacting me? The effective helper is a reflective helper, always contemplating whether there are better ways, or how one might do things differently (Winfield, 2005). As the practitioner intervenes in the moment, they are questioning why they are doing what they are doing. After the intervention is over, the practitioner reviews why they did what they did. In preparing for the next intervention, one might ask: 'Why am I thinking of doing this?' 'What is influencing me to think like this?' or 'How might my various actions be interpreted by the other person(s)?' This continuous process of reflection before, during, and after an action (Schon, 1983) helps the CYC practitioner to stay constantly focused, in an ongoing way, on acting in the best interests of the other(s).

Doing

> *"Professional involvement is about doing with intention."*
> (Ricks, 1992)

Connection and Engagement builds from the notion that if someone is not connected with another, and/or if one cannot engage with them in a significant and culturally meaningful manner, then the practitioner's interventions cannot be effective (Garfat & Charles, 2010). It is unacceptable to blame the 'other' when they are nonresponsive; it is the practitioner's obligation to work towards making the connection. All too often, a failure to connect or engage gets rendered as a diagnostic justification for 'what's wrong with the other person'. Relationship is the foundation of all CYC work and connection is the foundation of relationship (Brendtro & du Toit, 2005). The practitioner connects with the person, and then engages with them as they live their lives. Helping a young woman nurse her child, assisting parents to prepare the garden, teaching a young person to shoot a basketball, helping a new immigrant to navigate the health and welfare systems, combating oppressive practices, etc. – all such engagements are powerful when one is connected in relationship *with* another and sometimes with community.

Rituals of Encounter require that Child and Youth Care practitioners give conscious reflection to the ways in which they engage with another. This involves giving respectful attention to important protocols associated with engaging with someone from cultural traditions that are different from one's own (Fulcher, 2003). It also means paying attention to one's own positionality, particularly when practitioner and young person represent different races, faith groups, gender identities, etc. Simply trying to understand, as well as contemplate different relational starting points can present major challenges. One's own personal experiences of acculturation and socialisation impose taken-for-granted assumptions and a cognitive mindset that is not easily altered. Rituals of encounter between practitioner(s) and children or young people have developed through cultural protocols. The meaning a young person gives to culture – including youth group or gang culture – is constantly evolving as they seek to understand and adapt to their current situation and any new living environment or experiences. Each encounter requires that a cultural lens be included in a CYC practitioner's basic competencies. Like transitional objects, rituals of encounter strengthen purposeful communication. And for each person, from each culture, it is unique.

Ritual is important to identity formation and to our existence as social beings. From daily routines to the ways we meet and greet each other, rituals place us with one another, bringing us together by framing shared experiences; helping us to recognize self in each other. Rituals can also be a way of showing *resistance to injustice*, a way of contesting power through a public celebration of common purpose (Snell, 2017).

Intentionality means that everything a Child and Youth Care practitioner does is done with a purpose (Molepo, 2005). There are few 'random' actions or interventions. It means thinking consciously about *what is required for the other to be comfortable* with intentional attempts at making connections. All the practitioner's interventions are planned and fit with the regularly reviewed goals established with the young person and/or their families. When a community-based CYC practitioner meets with a family in their home, it is important to decide how each individual will be greeted on arrival, who will be greeted first and how one will be with them. All of these decisions, as a reflective practitioner, take into consideration the similarities and differences between the practitioner and other – culture, race, identity, place in the world, etc. A CYC practitioner facilitating a training program, for example, needs to decide how the group will be greeted, how individuals might be singled out for attention, how the practitioner needs to open themselves to the differences between themselves, as the trainer, and the identities of the participants. No matter where CYC practitioners work, what they do is always intentional and contextually considered. This does not mean that one abandons spontaneity. But even in the moment of spontaneity, the practitioner continues to reflect on their intention(s) in the moment. As Ricks, 1992, p. 56) said, "the intentional involvement in intervention requires that the worker be thoughtful and have clarity of purpose in determining "what to do before doing it". This is the core of reflective practice.

Meeting Them Where They Are At. Meeting people 'where they are at' (Krueger, 2000) involves being with people where they live their lives but also more than that. It means accepting people for *how they are* and who they are as we encounter them in their lives. They may be 'different' from us and we must honour and adapt to that difference. It means responding appropriately to their developmental capabilities, accepting their fears and hesitations, celebrating their joys and enabling them – without pressure – to be who they are in interactions with others (Small & Fulcher, 2006). It also means that we must be open to their suspicions of us, their perceptions of how we are different, and their hesitations to engage or be engaged. Young people and families from traumatized, racialized or transgender communities have good reason to be weary of anyone presenting themselves as 'helpers'. This is important (and perhaps even more so) when the 'differences between us' make us afraid or uncomfortable. As Krueger said, we must be "geared to their emotional, cognitive, social, and physical needs" (2000, n.p.). Just as a forest guide must meet others at the beginning of their journey, so does the CYC practitioner meet the other "where they are at" as they begin the journey and then move on together from there. Meeting people where they are at also requires that the practitioner be aware of the circumstances that brought them there.

Purposeful Use of Activities. Phelan (2017) has argued that one of the essential tasks of Child and Youth Care practitioners is to arrange experiences for people. The practitioner arranges "experiences that promote the possibility of new beliefs for the people we support" (Phelan, 2009, n.p.). The practitioner attempts to facilitate learning opportunities in the everyday. Such learning opportunities and the purposeful use of activities enable children and young people to experience safer places where new experiences can happen, and important learning can be nurtured. One learns about and takes into consideration a person's previous experiences in anticipation of how new experiences might offer the potential for growth (Phelan, 2009, n.p.). For example, someone who has never experienced being cared for may experience this through a learning opportunity and planned experience arranged – even engineered – by the CYC Practitioner. As Karen VanderVen (2003) has said, the purposeful making of a water bomb with a balloon or making a meal together can change a life.

Doing 'With', not 'For' or 'To' refers to how CYC practitioners engage with people, helping them to learn and develop through doing things *with* them. In this way we do not deny them the prospect of learning and growing through doing everything for them, especially when they are capable of doing it themselves (Delano & Shaw, 2011). Nor does one stand back and do things to them (such as ordering them about). Ultimately one remains engaged 'with' people through the process of their own growth and development, walking alongside them as a guide, acknowledging their similarities and differences. This process of 'doing with' requires the practitioner's ongoing commitment to the co-created space between practitioner and other, monitoring the changing characteristics and experience of that co-created space (Phelan,2009). Whether it is in supervision, with a family in a rural garden, or engaging in any other activity – the constant focus is on being and doing *with* the other. As Al Trieshman suggested in 1982 (n.p.), "When we do things *to* youth and not *with* them, it is not going to work so well".

The foregoing is not meant to imply that there are never times when we do things to, or for, young people and others. There are times and situations when a young person, for example, may not have the physical ability or capacity to do everything with the CYC practitioner. In these situations, the practitioner may indeed do some things 'for' the young person, while still being engaged *with* the young person, but only to the point where the young person is once again able to engage *with* the practitioner (dressing oneself comes to mind as an example). There are also times when it may be appropriate to do 'to' the young person – for example in situations of imminent and serious harm to self or others. However, always the goal is to return to a state of 'doing with' as soon as possible.

Doing with implies that we are engaged with them, even if we are doing something for them, which means that our doing for them is done in an agreed engagement. Indeed, if we have been engaged in doing *with* them, before the need to 'do to' arises, then *our doing to is in the context of doing with* and likely makes the process easier.

Independence – or perhaps better stated as inter-dependence – is a goal for many young people who want to live on their own. Doing with, for, or to is inherently tied to assessing and responding to developmental process and growth and individualized in each interaction of caring.

Rhythmicity refers to the shared experience of engaging in a synchronized, dynamic connection with another (Krueger, 1994; Maier, 1992). Rhythms of coming and going, rhythmic rituals of acknowledgement, patterns of play amongst children, simple repeated gestures of greeting at the door of the family home, special handshakes on the street, or with a teacher on entering the classroom – all are examples of the rhythms in which one might engage and experience with people. Connecting in rhythm with people helps to nurture and strengthen connections and a sense of 'being with' that person. We pay particular attention to the rhythms that acknowledge the ways of being and doing of young people, their families and communities, especially when working across racial, gender or other identities. While working, regardless of location, a child and youth care approach invites one to pay particular attention to the rhythms of that person's, or that family's life, thereby strengthening opportunities to enter into rhythms of connectedness and caring with them.

Being Emotionally Present. Mark Krueger was perhaps the greatest advocate in the CYC field for 'being present' (Krueger, 1999). Whether with children, young people or adults and families – being present remains a central feature of how CYC practitioners work. While difficult to describe, being present is an experience most will have had with another and in relations with other(s). Intentional presence is a core element of relational practice; the space in-between us cannot emerge, much less be recognized, unless we are present. At the same time, presence is not contingent on the practitioner's physical presence; we can be present virtually in the emotions, the imagination, or the mental constructions of the young person. No matter how we are present, it This involves allowing one's Self to be in the moment with the other or others (Fewster, 1990). At some level, of course, one is always 'present'.

But 'being present' in the relational sense involves the Child and Youth Care practitioner making a conscious effort to make her or his 'Self' available and self-evident in the moment, focusing with immediacy on the other(s). When I am with you, I am with you and not somewhere else! My thoughts and affections are connected in being with you in this moment. When I am unable to be physically with you, I leave in your presence a symbol of me, which could be what Henry Maier (1981) had termed 'a transitional object'. Ricks (2003) has argued that one of the most important aspects of relational practice is for the practitioner to be present with the other while simultaneously being present with self. She called this active self-awareness. As Ranahan (2017, p. 4) noted "when present – or presencing – child and youth care workers are fully implicated in the process in moments of naming and making visible silenced experiences".

Using Daily Life Events to Facilitate Change. Relational Child and Youth Care practice involves using the everyday, seemingly simple, moments which occur as CYC practitioners live and work with people to help them find different ways of being and living in the world (Maier, 1987). These moments – as they are occurring – provide the most powerful and relevant opportunities for change. Whether it be an opportunity-led event (Ward, 1998) with a child in a residential program or foster home, a life altering moment in working with a family (Jones 2007; Shaw & Garfat, 2004), a brief encounter with youths on the street (Apetkar, 2001), or a simple exchange in a rural college classroom (Shaw, 2011) – the moment, and it's potential for powerful change, is seen as central to a CYC approach. Child and Youth Care practitioners are defined in their work by the way they make use of these moments.

Conclusion

The field of Child and Youth Care has expanded beyond its origins in residential child care to encompass youth work and a wide range of practices within child and youth services. Child and Youth Care practitioners are found everywhere – from the most isolated rural Isibindi projects in South Africa, to the halls of college and university academia. Practitioners can be located using a CYC approach from the streets of large urban cities to isolation wards in children's hospitals; and from the tundra of northern Canada to the mountains of Bulgaria or Borneo. It is a worldwide practice – especially across the English-speaking world that parallels the European tradition of Social Pedagogy.

Child and Youth Care practitioners can also be found working in non-English-speaking places where political and economic histories may have introduced English patterns of health and social services administration. This includes places that are looking to

'English-speaking countries' for examples (for better or worse) of best practice in the delivery of health and welfare services for children, young people and their families. The activities of international non-governmental organizations have also contributed to the extension of Child and Youth Care approaches through recruitment of health and welfare personnel to provide care for children, young people and families in the so-called global South.

Experience in the field shows that a Child and Youth Care approach may find ready applications in direct care work with people of all ages across the life span of development, and in all settings (see VanderVen, 1992). As noted from the beginning, a Child and Youth Care approach represents a way of being and working in the world. Fundamentally, it is, about how one does what these practitioners do, not a question of what the practitioner is called or where they are located. It is this type of relational approach which gives us hope and the opportunity to be among the most influential of healers and caring individuals in a child or family's life.

References

Abraham, E. (2009). *Team parenting.* Bromsgrove, England: Foster Care Associates.

Ainsworth, F. (2006). Group care practitioners as family workers. In L.C. Fulcher & F. Ainsworth, (Eds). *Group care practice with children and young people revisited.* New York: The Haworth Press, pp. 75-86.

Aptekar, L. (2001). Cross-cultural problems faced by people who work with street children. Presentation made at HSRC Conference "Street Children: From resolutions to action". Retrieved from http://www.CYC-net.org/CYC-online/CYCol-0601-aptekar.html

Baizerman, M. (1999). How can you recognize a Youth Worker? *CYC-OnLine*, 11. Retrieved from http://www.CYC-net.org/CYC-online/CYCol-1299-youthworker.html

Bellefeuille, G. & Jamieson, D. (2008). Relational-centred planning: A turn toward creative potential and possibilities, In G. Bellefeuille, and F. Ricks, (Eds) *Standing on the precipice: Inquiry into the creative potential of Child and Youth Care Practice*, (pp 35-72), Alberta, Canada: MacEwan Press.

Bristow, Y. (2017). BIDing and autism. *CYC-OnLine*, 222, 18-22.

Brokenleg, M. (1998). Native wisdom on belonging. Reclaiming Children and Youth, 7(3), 130-132.

Brendtro, L. & du Toit, L. (2005) *Response ability pathways – Restoring bonds of respect*. Cape Town: Pretext Publishers.

Brendtro, L. & Larson, S. (2005). *The resilience revolution*. Bloomington, IN: National Educational Service.

Burford, G. E. & Fulcher, L. C. (2006). Resident group influences on team functioning. In L. C. Fulcher & F. Ainsworth, (Eds). *Group care practice with children and young people revisited*. New York: The Haworth Press, pp. 177-208.

Charles, G., Freeman, J. & Garfat, T. (2016). *Supervision in child and youth care Practice*. Cape Town: The CYC-Net Press.

Daniel, B. J. (2016). Building healthy communities and reducing crime: Communities of practice. In B. J. Daniel (Ed.), *Diversity, justice and community: The Canadian context* (pp. 243-258). Toronto, ON: Canadian Scholars Press.

Delano, F & Shah, J. C. (2011). Games played in the supervisory relationship: The modern version. *Relational Child and Youth Care Practice*, 24(1-2), 193-201.

deFinney, S., Loiselle, E., & Dean, M. (2010). Bottom of the food chain: The minoritization of girls in child and youth care. In A. Pence & J. White (Eds.), *Child and youth care: Critical perspectives on pedagogy, practice, and policy* (pp. 70-94). Vancouver, BC: UBC Press.

Digney, J. (2007). A time to laugh, a time to think, a time to act. *CYC-OnLine, 100*. Retrieved from http://www.CYC-net.org/CYC-online/CYCol-0507-digney.html

Fewster, G. (2005a). I don't like kids. *Relational Child and Youth Care Practice, 18*(3), 3-5.

Fewster, G. (2005b). Just between you and me: Personal boundaries in professional relationships. *Relational Child and Youth Care Practice, 17*(4), 8-17.

Fewster, G. (2004). Editorial. *Relational Child and Youth Care Practice, 17*(3), 3.

Fewster, G. (2001). Getting there from being here. *CYC-OnLine, 26* . Retrieved from http://www.CYC-net.org/CYC-online/CYCol-0201-fewster.html

Fewster, G. (1990). *Being in child care: A journey into self*. New York: Haworth.

Fletcher, J. (1998). Relational practice: a feminist reconstruction of work. *Journal of Management Inquiry, 7*, 163-186.

Freeman, J. (2015a). Trauma and relational care: Integrating an awareness of trauma into the characteristics of relational child and youth care. *Journal of Child and Youth Care Work, 25,* 120-132.

Freeman, J. (2015b). Lingering in the moment. *CYC-OnLine, 198,* 23 – 25. Retrieved from http://www.CYC-net.org/CYC-online/aug2015.pdf

Freeman, J. (2014). Organizational Accreditation: How Training on the Therapeutic Use of Daily Life Events Meets Behavior Support Standards and Promotes Relational Practice. *CYC-OnLine, 181,* 12-18.

Freeman, J. (2013). Recognition and naming of human strengths. *CYC Online, 177,* 7-11.

Freeman, J. & Garfat, T. (2014). Being, interpreting, doing: A framework for organizing the characteristics of a relational child and youth care approach. *CYC Online, 179,* 23-27.

Fulcher, L.C. (2003) Rituals of encounter that guarantee cultural safety. *Relational Child and Youth Care Practice, 16*(3) 20-27.

Fulcher, L.C. (2004). Programmes & praxis: A review of taken-for-granted knowledge. *Scottish Journal of Residential Child Care, 3*(2), 33-34.

Fulcher, L.C. (2006a). The soul, rhythms and blues of responsive child and youth care at home or away from home. In L.C. Fulcher & F. Ainsworth, (Eds). *Group care practice with children and young people revisited.* New York: The Haworth Press, pp. 27-50.

Fulcher, L.C. (2006b). It's only a matter of time: Cross-cultural reflections. *Relational Child and Youth Care Practice, 18*(4), 58-64.

Fulcher, L.C. & Garfat, T. (2008). *Quality care in a family setting: A practical guide for Foster Carers.* Cape Town: Pretext.

Fulcher, L.C. & Garfat, T. (2015). *Child and Youth Care Practice with Families.* Cape Town: The CYC-Net Press.

Fulcher, L.C. & Ainsworth, F. (2006). *Group care practice with children and young people revisited.* New York: The Haworth Press.

Gannon, B. (2008). The improbable relationship. *CYC On-Line, 110.* Retrieved from http://www.CYC-net.org/CYC-online/CYCol-0408-gannon.html

Gannon, B. (2014). Create positive moments. *CYC On-Line,118.* Retrieved from http://www.cyc-net.org/cyc-online/apr2014.pdf#page=11

Garfat, T. (1999). On Hanging Out. *CYC-Online, 8.* Retrieved from http://www.cyc-net.org/cyc-online/cycol-0999-editorial.html

Garfat, T. (2002). "But that's not what I meant": Meaning- making in Foster Care. *Irish Journal of Applied Social Studies, 3*(1), 113–124.

Garfat, T. (Ed) (2004a). *A Child and Youth Care approach to working with families.* Binghamton: The Haworth Press, Inc.

Garfat, T. (2004b). Meaning-making and intervention in child and youth care practice. *Scottish Journal of Residential Child Care, 3*, (1), 9-10.

Garfat, T. (2008). The inter-personal in-between: An exploration of Relational Child and Youth Care practice, In G. Bellefeuille, and F. Ricks, (Eds) *Standing on the precipice: Inquiry into the creative potential of Child and Youth Care Practice*, (pp 7-34), Alberta, Canada: MacEwan

Garfat, T. (2013). *Conference presentation*. 19th Biennial Conference. National Association of Child Care Workers. Presentation at the NACCW Conference. Cape Town, South Africa.

Garfat, T. (2015). Editorial: Trauma, Relational Safety and a Child and Youth Care Approach. *CYC-OnLine,198*, 4-5.

Garfat, T. (2016) Nudging the development of relational safety. *CYC-OnLine, 213*, 2-4.

Garfat, T. & Charles, G. (2010). *A guide to developing effective child and youth care practice with families*. Cape Town: Pretext.

Garfat, T. & Fulcher, F. (2012). Applications of a CYC Approach. *Relational Child and Youth Care Practice, 24*(1-2).

Garfat, T., L.C. Fulcher, & Digney, J. (2013). *Making moments meaningful in child and youth care practice.* Cape Town, South Africa: CYC-Net Press.

Gharabaghi, K (2009). Too complicated, too fast. *CYC-OnLine, 128*. From http://www.CYC-net.org/CYC-online/CYConline-oct2009-gharabaghi.html

Gharabaghi, K. (2014) Relationships and relational practice. *CYC-OnLine, 185*, 6-9.

Gharabaghi, K. (2016). Why are we so white? *CYC On-Line, 220*. Retrieved from http://www.cyc-net.org/cyc-online/jun2017.pdf#page=6

Gharabaghi, K. (2017a). It's a wonderful world (of CYC). *CYC-OnLine, 224*, 5

Gharabaghi, K. (2017b). A second language for every CYC. *CYC-On-Line, 222*, 12-15.

Gharabaghi, K. & Stuart, C. (2011). *Right Here, Right Now: Exploring Life-Space Interventions for Children and Youth*. Pearson, Canada.

Gilligan, R. (2009). *Promoting Resilience: Supporting children and young people who are in care, adopted or in need*. London: BAAF.

Gompf, K. (2003). Connecting while connecting the dots. *Relational Child and Youth Care Practice, 16*(2), 74-75.

Hill, M. (2001). Change is hard" And sometimes we make it harder. *CYC-OnLine, 26*. Retrieved from http://www.CYC-net.org/CYC-online/CYCol-0201-change.html

Hilton, E. (2002). Old programs and new. *CYC-OnLine, 39*. Retrieved from http://www.CYC-net.org/CYC-online/CYCol-0402-hilton.html

Hooks, B. (2000). All about love: New Vision. New York: Harper Perennial.

House of Commons Select Committee (2009). Children, schools and families, third report: *Looked after children*. London: Westminster.

InclusionBC. (2018). *What is inclusion?* Retrieved from http://inclusionbc.org/WhatIsInclusion

Jones, L. (2007). Articulating a Child and Youth Care Approach to family work. *CYC-On-Line, 104*. Retrieved from http://www.CYC-net.org/CYC-online/CYCol-0709-jones.html

Krueger, M. (1994). Rhythm and presence: Connecting with children on the edge. *Journal of Emotional and Behavioral Problems, 3*, 1. 49-51.

Krueger, M. (1999). Presence as Dance in Work with Youth. *Journal of Child and Youth Care, 13*(2), 69-70.

Krueger, M. (2000). Central themes in child and youth care practice. *CYC-OnLine, 12*. Retrieved from http://www.CYC-net.org/CYC-online/CYCol-0100-krueger.html

Krueger M. (2004). Defining relational work. *CYC-OnLine, 67*. Retrieved from: http://www.CYC-net.org/CYC-online/CYCol-0408-krueger.html

Krueger, M. (2006). Exploring Class and Critical Race Theory: Rethinking how we might have gone wrong in developing the profession. *CYC-OnLine, 95*. Retrieved from http://www.CYC-net.org/CYC-online/CYCol-0612-krueger.html

Krueger, M. & Stuart, C. (1999). Context and competence in work with children and youth. *Child and Youth Care Forum, 28* (3), 200-201.

Maier, H. W. (1979). The core of care: Essential ingredients for the development of children at home and away from home. *Child Care Quarterly, 8*(3), 161-173.

Maier, H.W. (1981). Essential components in care and treatment environments for children and youth. In F. Ainsworth, & L.C. Fulcher (Eds.). *Group Care for Children: Concepts and Issues*. (pp. 19-70.) New York: Methuen.

Maier, H. W. (1987). *Developmental group care of children and youth*. New York: Haworth Press.

Maier, H. W. (1992). Rhythmicity – A powerful force for experiencing unity and personal connections. *Journal of Child and Youth Care Work, 8*, 7-13.

Marshall, N. (2017). *CYC-Net Discussion Group* posting.

Mattingly, M. A. (2006). Managing occupational stress for group care personnel. In L. C. Fulcher & F. Ainsworth, (Eds). *Group Care Practice with Children and Young People Revisited*. New York: The Haworth Press, pp. 209-230.

Michael, J. (2005). Life-space supervision in child and youth care practice. In T. Garfat and B. Gannon, (Eds.). *Aspects of Child and Youth Care Practice in the South African context*. Cape Town: Pretext, pp.49–62.

Milligan, I. & Stevens, I. (2006). *Residential Child Care: Collaborative practice*. London: Sage Publications.

Mann-Feder, V., Scott, D., & Hardy, B. (2017). The future of child and youth care education: Insights from Canada. *International Journal of Child, Youth and Family Studies, 8*(2). Retrieved from https://journals.uvic.ca/index.php/ijcyfs/article/view/17722

Mann-Feder, V.R. (2011). Child and Youth Care work and talk therapy. *Relational Child and Youth Care Practice, 24*(1-2), p. 67-71

McCabe, G.H. (2007). The healing path: A culture and community-derived Indigenous therapy model. *Psychotherapy: Theory, Research, Practice, Training, 44*(2), 148-150.

Molepo, L. (2005). Working with youth and families affected/infected by HIV/AIDS within the South African reality. In T. Garfat, and B. Gannon (Eds.). *Aspects of Child and Youth Care practice in the South African context*. Cape Town. Pretext. pp. 63-74.

Mucina, D. (2012). Ubuntu: Sharing our Black knowledge with our children. *Relational Child and Youth Care Practice, 25*(4), 59-65.

Munroe, T. (2017). Enriching relational practices with Critical Anti-black Racism advocacy and perspectives in schools. *Relational Child and Youth Care Practice*, 30, (3), 32-45.

Naidoo, D. (2005) Reflections of my journey in child and youth care. *Journal of Child and Youth Care, 23*(1), 23

Phelan, J. (2009). The wounded healer as helper and helped: A CYC model. *CYC-OnLine*, 121. Retrieved from http://www.CYC-net.org/CYC-online/CYConline-mar2009-phelan.html

Phelan, J. (2017). *Intentional CYC supervision: A developmental approach*. Claremont, South Africa: CYC-Net Press.

Ranahan, P. (2000). Reaching beyond caring to loving in child and youth care practice. *Journal of Child and Youth Care*, 13(4),55-65

Ranahan, P. (2017). Deepening a child and youth care understanding of presence: Engaging living-dying dialectical moments. CYC-Online,217, 4.

Redl, F & Wineman, D (1952). *Controls from within*. Glencoe, IL: The Free Press.

Relational Child and Youth Care. (2011). *Applications of a child and youth care approach* [special issue], 24(1/2).

Ricks, F. (2003) Relatedness in Relationships: It's About Being. *Relational Child and Youth Care Practice, 16*(3) 70-77.

Ricks. F. (1992). A feminist's view of caring. *Journal of Child and Youth Care, 7*(2), 49–57.

Schon, D. A. (1983). *The reflective practitioner: How professionals think in action.* New York: Basic Books.

Scottish Journal of Residential Child Care (2017). Love [special issue], *15*(3).

Shaw, K. (2011). Child and Youth Care education: On discovering the parallels to practice. *Relational Child and Youth Care Practice, 24*(1-2), 176-180

Shaw, K. & Garfat, T. (2004). From front line to family home: A youth care approach to working with families. In T. Garfat (Ed) *A Child and Youth Care approach to working with families.* New York. Haworth. pp. 39-54.

Skott-Myhre, H. (2017). Seeking a Pass: White Supremacy and CYC. *CYC-OnLine, 200,* 12-17.

Small, R. W. & Fulcher, L. C. (2006). Developing social competencies in group care practice. In L. C. Fulcher & F. Ainsworth, (Eds). *Group Care Practice with Children and Young People Revisited.* New York: The Haworth Press, pp. 51-74.

Smart, M. (2006) The Carberry project. *CYC-OnLine, 87.* Retrieved from http://www.CYC-net.org/CYC-online/CYCol-0406-carberry.html.

Smith, M. (2011). Love and the CYC relationship. *Relational Child and Youth Care Practice, 24*(1-2), p. 205-208

Snell, H. (2017). The ritual of practice. *Relational Child and Youth Care Practice, 30*(2), 3-5

Steckley, L. & Kendrick, A (2008) Hold On: Physical restraint in residential child care. In A. Kendrick, (Ed.) *Residential child care: Prospects and challenges.* London: Jessica Kingsley Publishers, pp. 152-165.

Steckley, L. & Smart, M. (2005). Two days in Carberry: A step towards a community of practice. *Scottish Journal of Residential Child Care, 4,* 2. Aug/Sep 2005. pp. 53-54.

Stuart, C. (2009). Foundations of Child and Youth Care, Dubuque: Kendall Hunt Publishing Company.

Thomas, N. (2005). *Social Work with young people in care.* Basingstoke, Hampshire, England: Palgrave Macmillan.

Thumbadoo, Z. (2011). Isibindi: Love in Caring with a Child and Youth Care Approach. *Relational Child and Youth Care Practice, 24*(1-2), 210-216

Thumbadoo, Z. (2008). Exploring the role of community child and youth care workers in South Africa: Where to from here? *CYC On-Line, 116*. Retrieved from http://www.cyc-net.org/cyc-online/cyconline-oct2008-zeni.html

Trieschman, A. (1982). *The anger within*. [Videotape interview.] Washington, DC: NAK Productions.

Vachon, W. (2018). Child and youth care fragility. *CYC On-Line, 232*. Retrieved from http://www.cyc-net.org/cyc-online/june2018.pdf#page=14

VanderVen, K. (2003). Transforming the milieu and lives through the power of activity: Theory and Practice. *Journal of Child and Youth Care Work,19*, 103-108

VanderVen, K. (Ed) (1992). *Journal of Child and Youth Care, 7*(4) & *8*(1) pp. vii-viii.

Ward, A. (1998). A model for practice: The therapeutic community. In Ward, A. & McMahon, L. (Eds.). *Intuition is not enough: Matching learning with practice in therapeutic child care.* London and New York. Routledge. pp. 70-71.

Whitfield, C.L. (1989). Healing the child within. Deerfield Beach, FL: Health Communications, Inc.

Winfield, J. (2005). An exploration of reflection and reflective practice. In B. Gannon & T. Garfat, (Eds.). *Aspects of Child and Youth Care practice in the South African context.* Cape Town: Pretext.

Winfield, J. (2008). Being in the moment. *Child and Youth Care Work, 26*, 3.

* * *

Originally published in *CYC-Online*, Issue 236, pp 7-46.

3

Purposeful Use of Daily Life Events in Care

Leon Fulcher

Intervening with children and young people through participation in daily life events may at first appear simplistic and common sense. To some extent that's true. There is a lot which may seem simple and much interaction with a child or young person that involves common sense. When consciously engaging in daily life events with a child or young person in out-of-home care – indeed any child or young person – it is important for Carers to nurture rhythms of interaction that may promote developmental achievements by that particular child or young person. A daily life approach to caring is relational and builds from relationships in the everyday – during the quiet times and the frantic times; the together times and the alone times; during hard work and the leisure times. Opportunity events occur in 168 hours per week of daily life moments (24 hours x 7 days), and some moments can change a lifetime. Purposeful use of daily life events challenges us to think more pro-actively about how we engage with young people in daily life events and moments.

When 'taking stock' in the here and now about daily life events with a child or young person, think of the following questions:

1. *What opportunities might be provided through today's planned life event(s)?*
2. *Who might join in?*
3. *Where will our planned life event(s) take place and how will we get there?*
4. *When do the planned life events happen and when will they finish, with debriefing?*
5. *How might opportunities for learning from these planned life event(s) contribute towards this child or young person achieving particular developmental outcomes?*

What might a Planned Daily Life Event involve?

It is important to remember that purposeful use of Daily Life Events don't require that a Carer or child go somewhere. Opportunities are provided through Daily Life Events offered during a rain or snow storm, or as might be experienced through planning and preparing dinner with a special desert for a family member or friend. Daily Life Events which involve going somewhere are also important. A purposeful trip to the shopping market for food and personal sundries offers many relational opportunities. A family outing for a game of bowling or kite-flying offers other opportunities, along with a few laughs. A trip to watch the ball game your young person plays in, or their school dramatic production. The main thing to remember is that these aren't just random events. Daily Life Events have a flow about them, all revolving around the particular young person in out-of-home care assigned to your care and supervision. During the course of every week in every season, there are the everyday activities; the once a week activities; the special one-off events; and what may be called unplanned events. A child or young person experiences these events, not as a series of one-off photographs, but as an instant replay video. As the video of My Daily Life Events builds up, so does it also show something of what relational activities took place and with whom.

Who might participate?

A developmental care perspective is required when thinking about Daily Life Events that may used purposefully with children and young people of any age.. Developmental care builds from an appreciation for what child and youth care worker and scholar Henry Maier called *The ABCs of Child and Youth Development*: *Emotional Development of Affect*; **B**ehaviour *and Life Skills Development*; along with *Cognitive Development and Thinking* capabilities. All 3 historic traditions of scholarship on child and adolescent development are represented in *The ABCs of Developmental Care*. Care Planning must address emotional development (**Affect**), the development of life skills (**Behaviour**), and deep brain learning around how children and young people think and comprehend their worlds (**Cognition**) in order to make developmental achievements whilst in out-of-home care. Some Daily Life Events happen routinely while others are planned for specific reasons for this particular child or young person. It thus follows that the more careful one considers any child's developmental capabilities and aptitudes, the more carefully one might tailored Daily Life Events and learning opportunities with that child during their time in out-of-home care. The main thing is: Daily Life Events need to connect with the learning and developmental needs of each particular child or young person.

Where will these Daily Life Event(s) take place and how do we get there?

Carers and youth workers are reminded that there is much one can do using Daily Life Events in virtually every room of a house, as well as in the garden, parks and fields around where children and young people live and play. One doesn't have to 'go out' for important learning opportunities to be experienced through the purposeful use of Daily Life Events. This spatial dimension of planning can be usefully examined when noting every week or two what rooms in a residential care setting are commonly used by children, young people and adults, and which rooms are used less frequently. Before going somewhere, think of the home, grounds and neighbourhood where children and young people live. How might you nurture learning opportunities through more purposeful use of Daily Life Events there?

When do the Daily Life Events happen & when will they finish, with debriefing?

There is one sense in which Daily Life Events are happening all the time through the continuous flow of life. Once children or young people and their Carer(s) get into daily and weekly rhythms of caring, there is no real beginning and ending to the opportunity events available through the more purposeful use of Daily Life Events. In the article entitled It's Only a Matter of Time, Carers are encouraged to think about daily and weekly rhythms and routines, routines that are often driven by school terms. Opportunities arising through Daily Life Events at the weekend are invariably different from those during the week. If not, why not? Sometimes events happen without planning. These, too, require thoughtful responses not just reactions in the moment. Learning to use opportunity moments in Daily Life Events can offer valuable diversionary tactics that can help Carers move from one activity into another with minimal disruption. Words to a song learned at Play Group capture a theme of transition in Daily Life Events that works at home as well as at school!: "*Clean-Up, Clean-Up, Everyone, Everywhere. Clean-Up, Clean-Up, Everybody does their share!*"

How might this Daily Life Event contribute towards particular developmental outcomes being achieved by this child or young person?

As Carers and youth workers enter into daily life rhythms with children and young people, so they begin to anticipate what Daily Life Events might nurture particular life skills and aptitudes with this young person. Children and young people may seek involvement in Daily Life Events which stimulate different life skills. Joining a football team provides large muscle, cardio-vascular and respiratory exercise. It reinforces teamwork and dependability at practices and games. The same can be said for participation in arts and drama activities, or of participation in Scouting or Guiding activities. Whilst risk-assessment issues are always to be borne in mind, purposeful involvement in Daily Life Events help children and young people learn how to structure their time, to participate in individual and group activities, and to extend daily life competencies worth learning for the future. A physiotherapist might prescribe a particular health and fitness regime. In a similar vein, Carers purposefully employ Daily Life Events to assist children and young people to achieve particular developmental outcomes important to their future health and well-being.

Summary

Like I said, this isn't rocket science. It is more of an art form that Carers and Youth Workers employ in their work with children and young people, especially those living in out-of-home care. Carers and youth workers were encouraged to carry a handful of questions with them into their Daily Life Events of caring. These were:

1. *What might a Planned Daily Life Event involve?*
2. *Who might participate?*
3. *Where will these Daily Life Event(s) take place and how do we get there?*
4. *When do the Daily Life Events happen & when will they finish, with debriefing?*
5. *How might these Daily Life Events contribute towards this child or young person achieving particular developmental outcomes?*

Keeping these questions constantly in mind helps the Carer to be more pro-actively prepared for any Daily Life Event.

4

Reflections on Daily Life Events in Child and Youth Care

James Freeman

Making the most of every moment we have with a young person plays a significant role in our effort to promote their optimal development and growth. The effective use of daily life events requires a recognition and understanding of the potential which can open up in a single moment. It also requires the ability to respond to naturally occurring and created moments as they occur.

The intentional use of daily life events is a characteristic of a contemporary child and youth care approach (Garfat & Fulcher, 2012) and is a primary factor in increasing the quality of interactions with those we care about. Thinking about and preparing for the significance of moments positions both parents and child serving professionals to maximize the development and growth of a young person:

> In child and youth care, every moment is highly significant and has the potential to cumulatively contribute to the growth of [a young person]...it is the micro-interactions between child and caregiver (either parent or substitute) that set the tone for the quality, and hence the impact of the interaction. (Vanderven, 1991, p. 16)

To maximize the impact of these micro-interactions requires a foundation of knowledge and skills including an understanding of human behaviour and development, self-awareness, empathy, and communication. In the larger knowledge base of child and youth care practice, these skills are identified within the domains of relationship and developmental practice (Mattingly, Stuart, & VanderVen, 2010) and are present in both classic and contemporary application of professional competencies (Curry, Schneider-Muñoz & Carpenter-Williams, 2012). A commitment to valuing young people and respecting their strengths and differences is essential as well.

The following scenarios are moments I have experienced in working alongside young people. I share them to ignite further thinking about how we can all use small moments in daily life to promote the development of those we work with and care about. Following each scenario is a brief commentary describing some of the structure of the moment and the elements of the intervention process. The questions following each scenario are intended to promote further reflection and transfer of learning to your experience and work with young people and their families.

Kicked out of everywhere

"My name is Derik and I've been kicked out of every after school program in town. Now my stepmom is sending me to your program." These were the first words from 14-year-old Derik as I pulled up to his school to pick him up for his first day in our after school program. "Hi Derik", I replied. "We don't kick people out of our program. Would you like to get in?" I motioned for him to climb in the van with the others and his tough face broke a slight smile as he climbed into the van. On the second day, Derik showed up at my van door and said he'd rather be anywhere else than coming with me. I replied that I was glad to see him again. I thought at least he showed up at the van stop. It's better than having to search for him or call his stepmom and let her know he's missing. The third day he showed up and as he got in the van I put my hand briefly on his shoulder and said I was glad to see him.

This is an example of a naturally occurring moment that was used to intervene in a specific way with Derik. I believed that he needed assurance that he was welcome in this new place and would be accepted by new people in his life. This young man turned out to be one of the more challenging individuals in the after school program. I'm not sure that in the moment I realized the importance of this first exchange and those that followed (Garfat, 2012), but based on these exchanges we maintained a positive connection through some challenging times in the year that followed. I often wonder how much of that goes back to our first interactions and how we interpreted each other in those brief moments.

Questions for reflection: What might you have done differently in this moment? What thoughts or feelings would this moment have created in you? What feedback would you look for as you planned your next action?

Divorced

As I greeted 6-year-old Beth after her kindergarten class one fall day, she sighed and said, "Well, I'm divorced." When I asked what she meant, she went on to explain that her dad moved out yesterday and that she now lives with just her mom and sister. I could see the weight of the world resting on her shoulders. What could I possibly say that would be helpful? My first thoughts were "Maybe they'll work things out" (but I knew that wasn't likely) or "Well, he didn't divorce you" (but that's how she felt and there wasn't much value in invalidating her feeling). So, I knelt down next to her, asked if I could carry her backpack, and gave her a hug around the shoulders. I asked if she would like to sit for a minute on the grass together. It was a shared moment of time where we both felt the weight of the experience together.

As we sat, I sensed her regaining some composure. Part of me wanted to say, "Whatever happened this weekend, we're here for you today." But I didn't. There was something about that response that made us and her parents seem at odds. Rather, I said to her, "You know, there's a couple other counsellors back at the camp that will be excited to see you. Are you ready to go see them?" After a quick van ride back to the camp, I made sure she connected with one of the female counsellors and got engaged in a craft activity we knew she enjoyed. I later found out that she had not mentioned anything about her home situation at school that day. She had waited to be with someone she felt safe with to express her feelings. Or at least the moment lent itself to that.

There are two opportunities described here. First, the moment sitting together on the grass, which was a naturally occurring moment. There was also the created moment of connecting her to another counsellor and activity. My aim was to support her in the skill of handling change and disappointments in life – something we aimed to build in every young person in the program. It also supported her specifically by showing her that in spite of the change at home, the counsellors and friends she had at the program would be there for her.

Questions for reflection: What might you have done differently in this moment? What potential for future moments does this shared moment create? How would you gauge this young person's availability? What indicates that she might be responsive in this moment?

Maybe you should just kill me

Danny was always a handful; 9 years old, fast, curious, and quick-witted. His difficulties with attention and impulses made his days challenging at times. This was especially true in the middle of the noise and busyness of summer camp. We had spent the day at the beach and the bus had just pulled back into camp. As the custom was, everyone began to get off starting with the seats in the front and working toward the back. Danny and I were in the back. Suddenly, before I even realized what happened, Danny had given in to his impulses, stripped off his clothes, and ran to the front of the bus shouting, "Me first! I want to change first!" I knew he was uncomfortable in his beach clothes and I should have been more prepared for what was about to happen. Catching up with him – after he ran streaking through the lobby full of other staff, kids, and parents – I found him crying in the changing room. He began to hit himself in the head, shouting and grunting. "I'm so bad, maybe you should just kill me," he said, looking straight into my eyes. I knew Danny and I knew this was a pattern for him. He often gave in to his impulses, sometimes taking things, sometimes pushing someone out of his way, and today running off the bus without clothes. After these impulsive behaviours, he would become overwhelmed with guilt and self-hatred. Based on my experience with him, I knew it was not a threat to take his life. So, I said, "Danny, you've got the right idea to get off the bus and get changed, we just need to find another way to do it." He looked at me confused as I explained that I understood what he had tried to do – to follow the agenda and get changed before snack time. He was so used to people telling him he was doing things wrong that when I told him he was right, it opened up the moment to work through what to do next time he wants to get off the bus in a hurry, without the humiliation and guilt he felt this time.

Although his behaviour may have been unpredictable in the moment, the opportunity was created (following him to the changing area) and specific to him (the staff had previously met together to design a coordinated and consistent response). The aim was to get him thinking positively about himself and helping him see that he had some sense of control over his actions.

Questions for reflection: What might you have done differently in this moment? How would you go about making sure you are connected with this young person in the moment?

I just wanted to run away

Jackson was the first kid to spit in my face. He was just 10 and as he tried to run into the busy street behind our facility, two of us physically stopped him. He was highly anxious and frustrated from an interaction that had occurred during a game he was playing with others. As we redirected him back to an area away from the street, we sat down on each side of him. Still highly escalated, he turned and spat right in my face. I could feel my impulses coming. Should I walk away? Should I hold him tighter? "We're not leaving you alone," I said in a quiet voice, hoping it would be comforting and some form of support to him. Sitting together for a few minutes, Jackson slowly began to breathe at his normal rate and his body relaxed. "I was so angry I just wanted to get away," he said. As we talked briefly about his conflict and ways he could handle it next time, I wondered what the impact of that moment would be.

This moment highlights the importance of awareness and use of self (Garfat & Charles, 2012). His speedy de-escalation was, in part, made possible through the existing connection we had established with him. Perhaps the impact of this moment for Jackson was one more piece of evidence that when he was feeling his worst, he would not be left alone.

Questions for reflection: What might you have done differently in this moment? How might this young person interpret physical intervention in this moment? What future moments might be planned to further support this young person?

Conclusion

Making the most of every moment we have with a young person plays a significant role in our efforts to promote their optimal development and growth. Understanding the potential of daily life events, and continuing to develop the skills to respond to naturally occurring and created moments will help us maximize the opportunities each moment brings in the life of a young person.

References

Curry, D., Schneider-Muñoz, A. & Carpenter-Williams, J. (2012). Professional child and youth work practice – Five domains of competence: A few lessons learned while highlighting the knowledge base. *Journal of Child and Youth Care Work.* 24, 6-12.

Garfat, T. (2012) Saying hello. In T. Garfat & L. C. Fulcher & J. Digney (Eds), *Readings for the therapeutic use of daily life events* (35-38). Cape Town: Pretext Publishing.

Garfat, T. & Charles, G. (2012). How am I who I am? Self in child and youth care practice. In T. Garfat, L. Fulcher & J. Digney (Eds), *Readings for the therapeutic use of daily life events* (44-66). Cape Town: Pretext Publishing.

Garfat, T. & Fulcher, L. C. (2012). Characteristics of a Relational Child and Youth Care Approach. In T. Garfat & L. C. Fulcher (Eds), *Child and Youth Care in Practice* (5-24). Cape Town: Pretext Publishing.

Mattingly, M., Stuart, C. & VanderVen, K. (2010). *Competencies for professional child and youth work practitioners.* Milwaukee: Association for Child and Youth Care Practice.

VanderVen, K. (1991). How is child and youth care work unique and different from other fields? *Journal of Child and Youth Care.* 5(1), 15-19.

* * *

Originally published in *Relational Child and Youth Care Practice*, 2013, Vol 26(2), 17-20

5

Exploring self to be with other: Relationship in action

Grant Charles and Thom Garfat

"Perhaps the key relationship to be considered, is our own relationship with our self" – (Ward, 2010, p. 65)

Self is central to making moments meaningful in Child and Youth Care Practice. Research by Stuart and Carty (2006) identified self not only as central to the domains of practice but suggests that self is the context for all our work. As the literature of our field has indicated for some time, the effective Child and Youth Care practitioner has an obligation to know self, to be aware of self, and to understand the role of self in the therapeutic relationship with others (Fewster, 2001b; Ranahan, 2000; Ricks, 2006).

Knowing self is not a tool, a technique or a strategy. It is a way of being; being in awareness, being present. The purpose of knowing self is so that one might be, and be with, self in the encounter with other. For it is only in the experience of being with self that we find the opportunity to genuinely connect with other (Fewster, 2001b). When one experiences genuine connectedness in an encounter with another human being, the door is opened for an alternative way of being and relating in the world; a way of being in relationship that includes being with self (Fewster,1990). Ironically, we can only find our true individual self in interaction with other, in the vulnerable context of an intimate relationship (Fewster, 2001a; McKeen & Wong, 2005; Ricks, 2001).

Frances Ricks (2001, n.p.) said that 'without self, there is no other' and Brian Gannon (2007, n.p.) has said, 'I am a person only in relation to other people'. We need to appreciate this interplay between self and other; this mutual co-creation of self. We become who we are through our relationships with others and they become who they are in relationship with us. It is impossible not to be in relationship.

While there are many factors that influence the quality and type of our interactions, we are constantly engaging with others in our environment (Charles & Charles, 2003). It is through these bi-directional relationships that we construct meaning in our lives (Alexander, 2008 ; Alexander & Charles, 2009; Valsiner, 2000). It is through this construction of meaning that we grow and change while constantly redefining who we are in the moment. Only through the acceptance of this mutuality with other can we truly know ourselves. This is one of the apparent paradoxes of our field (Garfat, 1999). Self and other are inseparable in relational Child and Youth Care practice. As Ward (2010, p64) has said, what is important is that we always consider "self in relation to others".

What is meant by "self"?

"What is self"? What do we mean by the word self? The word permeates our everyday life discussions. "I'll do it my-self"; "He is lacking in self esteem". "She is self-ish". "A worker should be self-aware". "Self-directed, self- involved, self and other". In the course of an average day, we may use the word self, standing alone or in conjunction with other words, a dozen times; or perhaps a hundred.

But how often, we wonder, do we actually pause for a moment and ask our selves (there it is again), "what is self?" Not often enough. Yet attending to self is essential if we are to attend to other (Krueger, 2007).

How we think about self is very much defined by the cultural codes of the time and context within which any discussion occurs. Your definition of self, whatever it may be, is contextualised by your culture, your time, your history, your experience, your family and many other things.

It was not that long ago when any writing in our field ignored the presence and role of self, except perhaps to make superficial comments about self-control, self-care or self-safety. Yet today any review of the literature reveals a concern with the essential self of the worker and youth or families. As the field has become more concerned with reflective practice (Dolan, Canavan & Brady, 2006; Garfat, 2005; Guttmann, 1991; van Weezel & Waaldijk, 2000) attention to self has become central to the effective helping process in all aspects of the system from service design to delivery. Self, then, has taken center stage in Child and Youth Care. As Stuart & Carty (2006, p. 71) said, in identifying the seven essential domains of competency, "self is seen as foundational to Child and Youth Care practice".

In its fullest form this self is more than physical, more than emotional, and more than cognitive. It is the sum total of all our aspects, and more. (Fewster, 2001b)

Gerry Fewster is perhaps the most profound and prolific of writers about self in our field. He argues that self exists at the core of our experiencing. Some might say that self is not only the core of our experience, but also of our existence, the centrality of that which we are. Frances Ricks (2001) argues that it is the self which is the individual lens through which we perceive and interpret all of our experiences. In the absence of an active awareness of self, one cannot know if what one experiences is 'real' or simply a projection of self on to other; a self-construction of other which may, or may not, have a basis in any objective reality of who the other 'really' is (Garfat, 1998). Self, then, is active, constant, and ever present.

When we talk like this about self, it is as if we are talking about something separate, distinct in some way, like when we talk about my brain, or my kidney. Yet the writing in our field suggests that self is not a separate thing. This of course is where any discussion of self begins to get complicated. If we talk about self, for example, who or what is talking, or making the observations? How can I talk about me, as if somehow the speaker and the thing about which is being spoken are different? As Ward (2010) has wondered "If *I* am using my self what does this imply? Who, or what is selecting and employing the self?" (p.54). How can I reflect on self, if, in fact, I am self? And maybe, in the end, that is the best definition there is. Self is who we are. Self is the answer to the question, "who am I?"

"Who am I?" is one of the most fundamental reflective questions for the Child and Youth Care practitioner (Garfat, 1998). With time and experience in this field, one encounters situations which demand that one explore, in depth, the centrality of their being. The question of the real or authentic self becomes more and more important as one progresses through various stages of development as a Child and Youth Care professional (Phelan, 1990). Of equal importance to us are the questions: "who do I appear to be to others?" and "how can I discover more about my self?"

On the presentation of self

"Workers bring self to the moment ..." (Krueger, 2007)

It has always been important to address the 'presentation of self' in our work with young people and families. In the early development of our field, the concern about how we presented ourselves was focused on such issues as appearance, general conduct and the like. At the time of hiring, for example, Child and Youth Care workers were screened to ensure they held 'proper' values, told what was 'appropriate dress' and monitored to ensure their conduct was reflective of mainstream values and practices. These values and practices were reflective of the dominant societal views at the time (Charles & Gabor, 2006) and how we presented ourselves was very carefully determined and monitored by the organisation for which we worked. Our concern with self was mostly limited to how you looked and acted, on the outside. Self was not really a well-developed concept in our field.

In contemporary Child and Youth Care literature the term 'the presentation of self' has taken on a different meaning involving how the values, beliefs, and characteristics of the individual worker show up in their interactions with youth, families and the other staff with whom they work.

A Johari Window

	Known to self	Not known to self
Known to other	*Open*	*Blind*
Not known to other	*Hidden*	*Unknown*

Imagine a Child and Youth Care worker who values family and believes that family is the most appropriate place for a young person to live and grow. This worker, whether in interactions with the youth and family, in case discussions, in team meetings, or any other aspect of her work, will manifest this belief through expression and action. In an individual interaction, for example, the worker will make reference to family, either implicitly or explicitly. In case discussions, she will constantly ask questions about family and perhaps try to move the plan towards keeping the youth at home. In team meetings, she will be a constant advocate for family inclusion. We see, then, that the values one holds position one to adopt a certain stance and to act in a certain manner.

Whatever she thinks this is her presentation of self – this is her self manifesting in the work environment. Who we are shows up in how we are (Ricks, 1989). Thus it is imperative that we know our own values and beliefs, our characteristics, our attitudes, our way of making sense of things. They impact on our every decision in ways we might not even notice.

What we know and what we don't know

"Becoming aware of how our beliefs, values, and ethics impact on us personally, we can also become aware of how they impact on our presentation to our clients." (Elsdon, 1998)

Ironic as it may seem, it is probably impossible to ever fully know our selves. There are some things we know about ourselves, and some things we don't know (Garfat, 1993). There are some things other people know about us, and some things they don't know about us.

Joseph Luft (1969) introduced the Johari Window as an exercise to demonstrate the importance of discussion and feedback in developing open communications. The diagram below is an example of the Johari Window.

Some things are known to Self, and some things are not. Some things are known to Other, and some are not. Let's look at the Johari Window components for a moment in the context of a Child and Youth Care practitioner with a family.

Open refers to those things *known to self and known to other*. This might include such things as physical characteristics of family members; the fact that the young person has broken the law; that the parents are not living together; that the mother is unemployed; etc. It may also include things about the worker like where she works, how old she is, her previous experience, depending on what she has disclosed to the family. In other words, things about which we all have knowledge.

Hidden refers to things which may be *known to self but not known to other*. In terms of our work, it may include such things as the father is having an affair (he knows it but no-one else does), the youth is involved with prostitution or the young person fears the father because of previous abuse. For the worker, it may include things like the fact that she is making her first home visit, that she is living common-law with a man with a criminal record or that she is hoping to leave early. The hidden area then covers areas which, at least for the moment, are not known to other. It also includes, of course, the myriad of values and beliefs which one person holds and is not, for whatever reason, disclosing to the other.

Imagine an interaction between a worker and a young woman and her family after they have been working together for three months.

- What are some of the types of things that the worker may know about herself, which would be unknown to the others?
- What are some things the youth might know about herself, which would be unknown to the worker?
- What are the types of things that might generally stay hidden in such a working relationship?

Blind refers to things that are *known to other, but not to self*. At first glance this may seem strange but a moment's reflection shows us that there are many things that other might know and of which we remain unaware. In a family meeting a parent may notice that the worker is speaking fast, but the worker may not be aware of it or the worker may notice that the mother always glances at the father before answering a question, a behaviour of which the mother may not be conscious.

Unknown refers to things which are *unknown to self and unknown to other*. It may be hard to believe that there could actually be things about ourselves that are not known to even ourselves. Imagine, however, that when you were very young you used to visit your grandmother, and when you were there you felt relaxed and special because she paid a great deal of attention to you. Now, years later, somewhere inside of you, you have a special feeling about grandmothers. You don't notice it, you certainly don't think it is abnormal, but there is a part of you that believes that grandmothers are good for young people. As a result of this experience with your grandmother and unknown to yourself and unknown to other, you may find yourself always exploring the possibility of a stronger connection between the young person and their grandmother.

On blind spots & blank spots

This area of known and not known is affected by how we pay attention to things. For example, if you notice some things and I do not, then this increases the area in which some things are known to you but not to me. We all focus differently during the course of our experience, even if we share the experience together.

We all walk through the world with what have been called "blind spots and blank spots" (Wagner, 1993). "*Blank spots* are those areas in which we know that we need to know more. *Blind spots. . .* are areas in which our current theory, method, or perceptions prevent us from seeing something as clearly as we might if we didn't have that blind spot... they represent areas in which we need to know more but we don't know we need to know more" (Garfat, 1993, p. 5). Knowing our blind and blank spots is an important part of the self-awareness of effective Child and Youth Care workers. Without this awareness, we see only a portion of what exists and think it is the whole. This lack of awareness can have negative consequences for those around us. For example, if we are unaware of a bias towards certain people we may treat them poorly without being fully aware of it.

We all see, as Frances Ricks (1989) said, through our own personal lens. It is as if we arise in the morning and don our own particular pair of glasses, and through these glasses, different than those of anyone else, we experience the world as we encounter it. That lens, like it or not, filters in some information and filters out other information. So, even though we have the experience together, some of it is known to you, some to me, and, quite frankly, some to neither of us.

Being knowledgeable about self

"Work with youth is a process of self in action" (Krueger, 1998)

Awareness of self is essential if the Child and Youth Care worker is to be able to distinguish self from other (Garfat, 2004; Mann-Feder, 1999); so that she might know, as Fewster (2001b) has said, 'where I end and the child begins'. Now this might seem a bit confusing. After all, as we stand facing one another, it seems clear to me that I am here and you are over there. We are after all, two separate entities; two separate beings are we not?

When you look at another person, what is it that you actually see? You see their physical presence; perhaps you see what they are doing. Let's go a little farther.

> *Imagine that you are approaching a young person to talk to her. You notice how she is standing, how her head moves, small gestures she makes. You notice the colour of her hair, the style of dress she wears, her jewellery and make-up. You watch and see how she responds as you approach her: perhaps she takes a half step backwards, looking around her.*

> *You conclude from everything that you have seen so far, that she is a member of a particular sub-group of adolescent society, that she is anxious about your approach, that she is not sure about adults.*

The first paragraph above was about the young woman. The second was about you. As we take in information, there is a natural human need to make sense of it, to interpret it, to make meaning from what we experience (Bruner, 1990, 2002). That is what was going on in the last paragraph.

> *As you continue to approach the young woman, you take into consideration your thinking that she is anxious. So you slow down a little, perhaps making eye contact, trying to assure her that you are not a threat. When you are within an appropriate distance, you speak softly, telling her your name and why you were approaching her. Your judgement is that if she knows why you are approaching her, she may relax a little, taking the first step towards trust.*

Once again, we would argue, your actions are all about you. You are acting on your interpretations, your 'best guesses'. This is what happens when we interact with people. *We interpret what we experience, and based on that interpretation, we act* (Garfat, Fulcher & Digney, 2012). But not all of us interpret and act in the same way to the same situation. Any one of us, approaching the same woman and seeing the same things, might respond differently. We might interpret, for example, that her behaviour is not a sign of feeling threatened, but is rather an invitation to come closer. But we also wonder 'what else might her actions be saying?'

Why is it that we interpret things differently? Where are these interpretations coming from, and how are they created? What influences us to perceive and interpret in a particular way? The answer is that we experience and act differently because of who we are and how we are different from each other.

We each create for ourselves through the course of time, history and experience, our own particular way of perceiving and experiencing. How we perceive and experience is influenced by a number of factors, including:

- Our values and beliefs,
- Our previous experiences in similar situations,
- Our theoretical knowledge,
- Our cultural experiences,
- Our gender and age,
- The characteristics of our up-bringing,
- The particular needs which are present at the moment.
- Our differing history of interactions with others and other systems.

From these we develop a way of perceiving, interpreting and interacting with the world and those we encounter. Take the example of how the young woman looked around as we approached her. We see her do this and we need to make sense of it.

Now imagine that once before you approached a different young woman and she did the same thing. As you talked to her, she looked around and two men stepped out of the shadows and told you to leave. You felt threatened and frightened. In retrospect, you think you were lucky to escape without physical harm. As you approach this new young woman and see the same action, your mind flips back to that previous experience and you wonder if the same thing is going on, if you need to be concerned for your own physical safety.

You notice that you are doing this because you are self-aware; because in your work, you are able to notice when you are making associations between this experience and the previous one. You are noticing, as you are walking, how you are responding internally to what you are experiencing. You notice your own anxiety and realise that it is coming from a previous experience. You separate out this lingering previous experience anxiety from the current situation.

This process of interpretation which is typically called meaning-making permeates all our actions and interactions. It is the process we go through whenever we engage with other and as we can see from the foregoing examples it can either help us connect or help us miss the mark. For if our interpretation of an experience or event is different than that of the young person with who we are working our interventions will likely be ineffective. Using the diagram below, let's look at a concrete example of how our personal process of making meaning may impact on the process of intervention.

For the purpose this example, let's assume that a young man is new to a residential program. In the program the boys rooms are on the first floor and the girls rooms are on the second floor. The boys are not allowed on the second floor under any circumstances.

John, the new boy, is wandering around the house getting to know the environment. As he does, he turns and puts his foot on the step leading upstairs. Sharon, the CYC worker, is on the far side of the room and sees him do this.

Sharon thinks that John is about to head upstairs because he has not learned the rules yet and in keeping with the team philosophy (peer influence) wants to help him avoid getting in trouble accidentally, so she raises her voice (cultural and family influence) and shouts across the room "I wouldn't do that!"

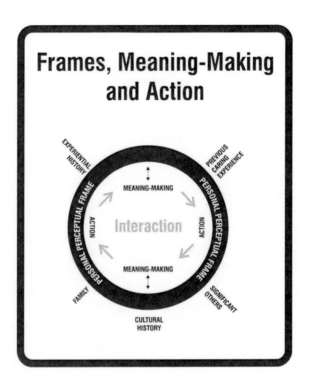

Frames, Meaning-Making and Action

MEANING-MAKING

Interaction

ACTION

MEANING-MAKING

EXPERIENTIAL HISTORY

PREVIOUS CARING EXPERIENCE

PERSONAL PERCEPTUAL FRAME

PERSONAL PERCEPTUAL FRAME

FAMILY

SIGNIFICANT OTHERS

CULTURAL HISTORY

John, hearing the worker shout at him thinks, based on his previous experiences with female adults, "She's yelling at me. Oh, no, I am in trouble already. I screwed up again." (personal history) Turning to Sharon and feeling that he needs to "defend" himself, shouts back at her: "I wasn't doing nothing!"

Sharon, based on her previous experience in similar situations, assumes he is about to escalate and so says to him, "It's okay. Calm down and come over here."

John has been in similar situations before, especially at home, when his mother would yell at him, call him over and when he got there she would hit him (previous caring experiences). He does not want to go through that again with this woman he does not know so, protecting himself, he snaps "Forget it! No way!"

*Sharon, now assuming John is about to escalate (previous experi-
ence, peer influence) moves towards him and signals to her
partner to come over.*

*John, seeing the gesture is reminded of when his mother called his
father into a situation (family) and how he would end up seriously
hurt. Based on his interpretation that the same thing is about to
happen, he yells "You can't touch me" and bolts from the program.*

*Sharon is left wondering what happened. She was trying to be
helpful and the next thing she knows she is dealing with a
run-away situation.*

We see in the forgoing example how we are influenced to interpret things in a certain way and then act on our interpretation.

One person acts, the other interprets, and then based on that interpretation acts in what they think is the appropriate manner.
This cycle repeats itself through the process of any interaction.

It is important in our work that we are actively aware of what is
going on for us, as it is going on. It is only then that we might tap
into our own process of interpretation and wonder how it is contributing to the interaction between us. This process of tapping
into ourselves is a part of the process of reflective practice (Garfat,
2005), which involves the worker making herself the object of her
own curiosity (Phelan, 2007).

One of our primary goals of working with people is to help
them to explore their self and how they structure their experience
of their lives. In order for us to be able to do this with youth and
families, we need to be able to do it ourselves.

On using or being self

*"... the "professional use of self": using one's own personal re-
sources (including one's own emotions as well as certain skills and
techniques) to achieve real communication. (Ward, 1998)*

The phrase the 'use of self' has become a important characteristic of our field. No-one seems really sure what it means and perhaps its purpose is simply to make us aware that self, your self, is the primary thing you have available in your work with young people and their families. But the way it is typically phrased, the use of self, makes it sound like the self is some kind of tool you have in your array of techniques; one which you whip out when the time is right and with it weave your magic of helping. Nothing could be farther from the truth. Self, and the encounter of selves, is, in fact, the essence of the helping relationship. By being truly self with other, we are in the condition of helping. In the earlier days of our field the use of self meant things like:

- Knowing when it was appropriate to self-disclose.
- Drawing on your own experiences to allow you to understand the experience of those which whom you were working.
- Noticing how you are feeling as a way of staying in touch with how others might be feeling.

Relational Child and Youth Care Practice, however, is more focused on 'being' self in relationship rather than 'using' self (Garfat & Fulcher, 2012). But, how can we 'be self' while in interaction with other? That seems the ultimate question, because the more that the other person experiences us as genuinely being ourselves with them, the more likely they are to want to enter in to a relationship with us that may be helpful to them. And the more likely they are to find their own 'self' while in that relationship. 'Being self' then is an invitation into relationship and to the 'in-between between us' (Garfat, 2008) which can only be created by the encounter of two selves in the moment of experiencing.

Being our self, does not mean doing whatever you want whenever you want to. It means that we are with other, complete with all our foolishness, fears, joys and curiosities, in a manner that genuinely reflects our inner, our whole, our genuine self, in response to being in relationship with other. That is being *I* in relationship *with* other (Austin & Halpin, 1987) and being self in relationship *for* other.

Closing comments

"It hardly requires a post modern leap to conclude, accordingly, that self is also other." (Bruner, 2002)

In the end there is only self. One cannot deny the presence of self, nor should one want to. If anything we seek just the opposite, to have self fully present in our interactions with others. But it is not the superficial self that we are seeking; not the shelled-self of everyday presentation, the cluster of defensive postures, positions and pretence that we so often hide behind in our daily lives. We are interested in the self that lays behind the daily posturing. We are interested in the genuine and profound self that is you as a human being. This self arises and is touched in rare moments of interaction with others. And the only way that self is going to be present when you work with young people and families, is if you work hard to know your self, to be aware of your experiencing as it is happening and to take the risks necessary to expose your self to yourself. For it is only when you truly know self, that you might know other.

References

Alexander, C. (2008). Reciprocity makes a difference. *Journal of Relational Child and Youth Care Practice*, 21(2), 27-35.

Alexander, C. & Charles, G. (2009). Caring, mutuality and reciprocity in social worker-client relationships: Rethinking principles of practice. *Journal of Social Work*, 9(1), 5-22.

Austin, D. & Halpin, W. (1987). Seeing "I" to "I": A phenomenological analysis of the caring relationship. *Journal of Child Care*, 3 (3), 37-41.

Bruner, J. (1990). *Acts of Meaning*. Cambridge, MA: Harvard University Press.

Bruner, J. (2002). *Making Stories: Law, Literature, Life*. New York: Farrar & Giroux.

Charles, G. & Charles, H. (2003). Guidelines in child and youth care family work: A case study. *Child and Youth Services*, 25(1/2), 95-115.

Charles, G. & Gabor, P. (2006). An historical perspective on residential services for troubled and troubling youth in Canada revisited. *Relational Child and Youth Care Practice*. 19(4), 17-26.

Elsdon, I. (1998). Educating toward awareness: Self-awareness in ethical decision making for Child and Youth Care workers. *Journal of Child and Youth Care*, 12(3), 55-67.

Dolan, P., Canavan, J. & Brady, B. (2006). Connecting with practice in the changing landscape of family support training. *Child Care in Practice*, 12 (1), 43-51.

Fewster, G. (1990). *Being in Child Care: A journey into self*. New York: Haworth.

Fewster, G. (2001a). Going there from being here. *CYC-Online*, Issue 25. Available here: http://www.cyc-net.org/cyc-online/cycol-0201-fewster.html

Fewster, G. (2001b). Turning my self inside out: my personal theory of me. *Journal of Child and Youth Care*. 15(4), 89-108.

Gannon, B. (2007). Self and others. *CYC-OnLine*. Available: http://www.cyc-net.org/cyc-online/cycol-0708-gannon.html

Garfat, T. (1993). On blind spots and blank spots. *Journal of Child and Youth Care*. 8(4) iii-iv.

Garfat, T. (1994). Never alone: Reflections on the presence of self and history on child and youth care. *Journal of Child and Youth Care Work*. 9(1), 35-43.

Garfat, T. (1998). The effective child and youth care intervention. *Journal of Child and Youth Care*, 12(1-2), 1-168.

Garfat, T. (1999). Questions about self and relationship. *Journal of Child and Youth Care*, 13(2), iii-iv.

Garfat, T. (2003). Four parts magic: The anatomy of a Child and Youth Care intervention. *CYC-OnLine*. Available at: http://www.cyc-net.org/cyc-online/cycol-0303 -thom.html

Garfat, T. (2005). Reflective Child and Youth Care Practice. *CYC-OnLine*. Issue 77. Available here: http://www.cyc-net.org/cyc-online/cycol-0605-editor.html

Garfat, T. (2008). The interpersonal in-between: An exploration of relational child and youth care practice. In G. Bellefuille & F. Ricks (eds), 7-34. *Standing on the Precipice*. Edmonton: Macwen Press.

Garfat, Digney & Fulcher (2012). 'The Therapeutic use of Daily Life Events (dle) training manual'. Cape Town: Pretext Publishing.

Garfat, T. & Fulcher, L.C. (2012). Child and Youth Care in Practice. Cape Town: Pretext Publishing.

Guttman, E. (1991). Immediacy in residential child and youth care: The fusion of experience, self-consciousness, and action. In J. Beker and Z. Eisikowits (eds) *Knowledge Utilization in Residential Child and Youth Care Practice* (pp. 65-84). Washington: CWLA.

Kostouros, P. & McLean, S. (2006). The importance of self-care. *CYC-OnLine.* Issue 89. Available here: http://www.cyc-net.org/cyc-online/cycol-0606-mclean.html

Krueger, M. (2007). *Sketching Youth, Self and Youth Work.* Rotterdam: Sense Publishing.

Luft, J. (1969). *Of Human Interaction,* Palo Alto, CA: National Press.

Mann-Feder, V. R. (1999). You/me/us: Thoughts on boundary management in Child and Youth Care. *Journal of Child and Youth Care.* 13 (2), 93-98.

McKeen, J. and Wong, B. (2005). To be ... Love-ing ... To be ... *Relational Child and Youth Care Practice,* 17(4), 61-62.

Phelan, J. (1990). Child care supervision: the neglected skill of evaluation. In J. P. Anglin, C. J. Denholm, R. V. Ferguson & A. R. Pence (Eds.). *Perspectives in Professional Child and Youth Care.* New York:Haworth.

Phelan, J. (2007). Curiosity and the ability to ask good questions. *CYC-OnLine.* Available here: http://www.cyc-net.org/cyc-online/cycol-0207-phelan.html

Ranahan, P. (2000). Reaching beyond caring to loving in child and youth care practice. *Journal of Child and Youth Care,* 13 (4), 55-65.

Ricks, F. (2006). Thus conscience does make cowards of us all: The need for moral courage in these times. *CYC-OnLine.* Available here: http://www.cyc-net.org/cyc-online/cycol-0507-ricks.html

Ricks, E (1989). Self-Awareness model for training and application in Child and Youth Care. *Journal of Child and Youth Care,* 4 (1), 33-41.

Ricks, F. (April 2001) Without the self there is no other. *CYC-OnLine* Issue 27. Available at: http://www.cyc-net.org/cyc-online/cycol-0401-ricks.html

Stuart, C. & Carty, W. (October, 2006). *The Role of Competence in Outcomes for Children and Youth: An Approach for Mental Health.* Toronto: Ryerson University.

Valsiner, J. (2000). *Culture and Human Development: An Introduction.* Thousand Oaks CA: Sage Publications.

van Weezel, L.G. & Waaldijk, K (2000). Being, acting, reflecting. *CYC-Online* Available at: http://www.cyc-net.org/cyc-online/cycol-1200-beact.html

Ward, A. (1998). *Intuition is Not Enough: Matching Learning with Practice in Therapeutic Child Care.* New York: Routledge.

Ward, A (2010). Relationship-based Social Work practice.

6

"If I'da thrown that chair at you, it woulda hit you': Seeing difficult behaviors through the lens of meaning and resilience

Stephanie Brockett and Ben Anderson-Nathe

This paper began in response to a call for proposals for a recent CYC International conference focusing on "inspiring resilience." We initially balked at the idea of submitting an abstract, raising doubts that resilience was something workers could (or should) inspire in youth. The ways we'd seen resilience treated in our own practice work felt nearly oppressive, like an expectation put upon young people without any real commitment from adults to support young people's choices and interpretations of their own lives. These concerns led to a series of interesting exchanges mostly concerning our reactions to the notion of resilience and how it fits in practice. Our own practice backgrounds have suggested to us that many youth in care demonstrate their own agency and resilience in daily events, with or without youth workers' attempts to inspire or facilitate resilience. The young person with an assault record, who in frustration throws a chair at the wall *near* a staff person, but deliberately does not throw it *at* that staff, we suggest, demonstrates resilience. Throwing the chair is problematic; it almost certainly violates the letter of the law in the residential placement. But the choice to exercise control and avoid an additional assault charge (throwing the chair at the wall, not the person) also illustrates a strength, an adaptation. That strikes us as resilient. Unfortunately, in most residential programs with which we have experience – most of which explicitly espouse a strengths-focused program philosophy – this behaviour would be constructed only as disruptive, dangerous, or otherwise inappropriate.

In this paper, we present a brief critique of common pitfalls in residential care, speaking most specifically to many programs' privileging behaviour modification and rule-compliance over opportunities for authentic relational engagement and facilitation of new insight with young people whose problematic behaviours may also demonstrate resilience and agency. Ungar (2004) articulates an understanding of resilience that we find useful for residential contexts, one that complements established notions of relational child and youth care practice: "the outcome from negotiations between individuals and their environments for the resources to define themselves as healthy amidst conditions collectively viewed as adverse," (p.342). Drawing on this conceptualization of resilience as the product of interactions between individual and environment, and Krueger's (1998) call for youth workers to attend to questions of meaning in relational practice, we suggest that problematic behaviours – everyday occurrences in residential care – can be reinterpreted as resilient, adaptive, and pregnant with possibility for deeper engagement with young people.

Residential care takes many forms depending upon locality, jurisdiction, treatment modality, precipitating event or intervention context, and more. The reflections that follow, and the interpretations and recommendations we make from them, are drawn largely from our experiences in the United States, where child and youth care is not yet a widely recognized or distinct profession, and residential workers receive little to no formal training or education to help frame their work. This is particularly salient in group homes for young people who are in the custody of the State, which are the focus of our reflections here. In most circumstances, these youth have not experienced great success with less restrictive environments (such as in-home supports, relative placements, or foster care) and come to residential care as a last-resort.

Our practice experience and much of the child and youth care literature points to a handful of common realities in residential care: reliance on point and level systems, a focus on treatment structured almost exclusively around behaviour modification and cognitive/behavioural restructuring, and assessing youth behaviours (particularly problematic ones) for future placements (Phelan, 2006; VanderVen, 2008; Vanderwoerd, 1991). In typical residential care programs, this behavioural control is enacted through point and level systems or token economies, thought to be effective because they are supposed to reward "positive" behaviours while not rewarding "negative" behaviours. In many point and level systems, youth earn points on a daily basis based upon enacting certain behaviours labelled as positive or desirable and avoiding those behaviours deemed problematic by the program. Far from facilitating new insight, shifts in residents' self-perception, or longstanding behaviour change, token economies often teach youth to jump through the hoops required of them in order to meet their treatment goals to move on (Abrams, Kim, & Anderson-Nathe, 2005).

Residential programs' focus on control arises at least partly in response to youths' behavioural bids for power in the residential setting (Arieli, 1997). The absence of a unified field of child and youth care in the U.S. creates a lack of educational opportunities (Fusco, 2012) for those working in residential care programs. This dearth of formal education leads some residential staff to default to control strategies which, although contrary to many central principles of relational practice, are nevertheless relatively easy to implement and consistent with familiar interventions in other related fields.

These point and level systems focus on daily life events, and in these events we think there is space for youth and staff to work together to facilitate new insight, shifts in youth self-perception, and longstanding behaviour change, when these small moments are held in a framework of resilience. Unfortunately, youth workers often receive explicit messaging from their programs to adhere to the expectations of the program structure even in circumstances where doing so interferes with authentic relationship or therapeutic growth for residents. Consider a young person who comes to residential care with a history of failed foster placements and destructive relationships (Brendtro, Brokenleg, & VanBockern, 1990/2002) and sneaks out of the house in the middle of the night to celebrate Christmas with a friend from school. He fully expects – based on a history in which this is true – that he will simply sneak back into his room in the morning before staff notice his absence. But when he is caught crawling through the window early the next day, staff response involves questioning his whereabouts, a urine analysis to test for drugs, and loss of privileges for violating the house rules. Far from learning that staff care enough to notice his absence, or that they are invested enough in him that they wonder where he went and validate the importance of this relationship in his life, the resident experiences a lose-lose situation, in which he is effectively punished for seeking out a meaningful relationship.

Many residential programs operating under these structures nevertheless pride themselves on their stated commitments to strengths-focused orientations to treatment or intervention and celebrate their commitment to fostering resilience among their residents. Seldom, however, do these programs articulate their functional definition of "resilience" or how the token economies central to their program structure reflect any genuine focus on strengths. We suggest that by explicitly adopting Ungar's (2004) conceptualization of resilience, programs can more meaningfully support and affirm the growth and new insight of their residents. Further, framing resilience in this way (as the product of individuals' interactions with their lifespace such that people can build self-definitions as healthy in spite of unhealthy circumstances) resonates well with Krueger's (1998) depiction of interactive youth work practice, in which the youth worker's responsibility is to hold ongoing and deliberate attention to the totality of the interaction between self, other, and place.

Although he cites four practice dimensions central to interactive and relational youth work, Krueger's (1998) emphasis on *meaning* links well with Ungar's (2004) interpretation of resilience. Youth workers' willingness to attend to the potential meanings of young people's behaviours represents one pathway by which youth can arrive at self-definitions that are healthy in spite of behaviours that might be interpreted as destructive. Krueger (1998) calls youth workers to attend to meaning at least in part by contextualizing young people's behaviours within their local, individual, and situational contexts, searching for the backstory to help make sense of behaviours that might otherwise be seen as simply oppositional. Gharabaghi (2008) has written about this in terms of recognizing and affirming fundamental notions of intersubjectivity – that youth and worker both carry their own past into the present, and relational practice demands that youth workers retain the perspective of past as it informs present conduct. In this context, workers strive to see through the behaviour itself, articulating instead the purpose and intention attached to youths' conduct. In the token economies and point and level systems that we have experienced, workers no longer positively engage in the lifespace of the youth, acting instead as judges of youths' behaviours independent of their historic or circumstantial context.

Opportunities abound for residential staff to interpret the everyday behaviours of young people as resilient and nested with meaning and significance, even as those behaviours may still be problematic. Take the case of Adam, a young person whose behaviour in the group home caused ongoing disruption to the program's daily structure. Adam would routinely threaten to destroy property around the house, to hurt himself, and to destroy the entire building. He became blustery and disruptive to the milieu, and staff found it increasingly difficult to meet their other obligations due to the time they had to spend de-escalating and providing consequences for Adam's conduct. Adam's behaviour was often interpreted as simply oppositional or conduct-disordered; staff responded accordingly with behaviour modification plans and consequences for disruptive behaviour. Missing from this conventional approach, however, was the recognition that

Adam's outbursts were learned behaviours from his home environment in response to perceived threats. In his home, Adam would frequently follow through by destroying property and eventually harming his sister. In the group home his lack of follow-through was, by our definition, an example of resilience. In offering empty threats, even in escalating those threats, without accompanying action, Adam offered a hint of the new insight and potential for new self-perception (as good and capable, in spite of adverse conditions). If staff understood the threatening behaviour in this context, these actions could also open a door for meaningful and potentially transformative conversations about Adam's past, present, and future that might otherwise have remained closed.

Alternatives to this punitive approach are endless. To begin, residential staff could support one another to attend, during Adam's threatening episodes, to the difference between his threats and his actual conduct. If threats that Adam might formerly have acted upon are no longer followed by problematic behaviour, workers can focus on the self-control Adam has demonstrated by simply threatening. Rather than responding with loss of privileges or deduction of points, these same staff might engage Adam in conversation about what strategies have helped him stop at threats, where he would formerly have acted on those threats. In this way, staff could help Adam reframe current behaviours in light of his past experiences, articulating what has changed in his environment, his relationships, and his own sense of agency. Outlining how similar behaviours served him in the past – in other circumstances – might help Adam gain insight into why he did the things he did then, which may no longer be necessary. In the past, for example, he might have destroyed things in response to being treated unfairly, or being told no, or as a way to get the adults in his life to pay attention to him. When those adults would react out of their own emotions, this underscored to Adam that people interact by being violent, that to get attention, one needed to be loud and explosive. When staff reframes Adam's behaviours in their appropriate context, they stand better prepared to support Adam in seeing the connections between his past and his present. This position opens the possibility for worker and youth to co-create alternative ways of getting the attention he needs without simply punishing Adam for the present behaviours, which only reinforces his notions of responding to violence with violence.

This and other applications of Ungar's (2004) concept of resilience highlight the importance of youth workers seeking out the many possible meanings of young people's behaviours. They also illustrate that it is critical for residential workers to understand and incorporate young people's histories into any interventions or programmatic responses to problem behaviours. Understanding how young people adapt to and make sense of themselves in context (both past and present), residential workers can reframe all behaviours, even problematic ones, through a lens of strength and adaptation. All behaviours serve a purpose for the young person (even if that purpose fails to match the program's goals), and can be used as a starting point in working with youth toward developing new skills, writing new stories, and setting the stage for the adoption of more pro-social interactions in the future. Further, this frame presents an alternative to many programs' rigid reliance on behaviour modification and compliance with point-and-level consequences or reinforcements. When youth and youth worker engage in dynamic relationship, attentive to making meaning of behaviours in the context of both past and present, possibilities open for youth to develop new insight and perspective. For the worker, it provides alternatives to simply consequencing behaviours that might actually reflect reasonable decision-making and harm reduction on the part of residents (as much as they still violate house rules). Reframing problematic behaviours, those daily life events in residential care, through the lens of resilience and meaning-making, holds the potential to enhance authentic and relational practice, benefiting youth, child and youth care workers, and residential settings themselves.

References

Abrams, L., Kim, K., & Anderson-Nathe, B. (2005). Paradoxes of treatment in juvenile corrections. *Child and Youth Care Forum. 34*(1), 7-25.

Arieli, M. (1997). *The occupational experience of residential child and youth care workers: Caring and its discontents.* Binghampton, NY: Haworth Press.

Brendtro, L., Brokenleg, M., & Van Bockern, S. (1990/2002). *Reclaiming youth at risk: Our hope for the future.* Bloomington: National Educational Service.

Fusco, D. (2011) *Advancing youth work: Current trends, critical questions.* New York, NY: Routledge.

Gharabaghi, K. (2008). Values and ethics in child and youth care practice. *Child & Youth Services, 30,* 185-209.

Krueger, M. (1998). *Interactive youth work practice.* Washington, DC: Child Welfare League of America Press.

Phelan, J. (2006). Controlling or managing behavior: A crucial decision. *CYC-Online. 86.*

Ungar, M. (2004). A constructionist discourse on resilience: Multiple contexts, multiple realities among at-risk children and youth. *Youth Society, 35,* 341-365. doi: 10.1177/0044118X03257030

VanderVen, K. (2008). When good people make bad things happen: The ten worst practices in child and youth work. *CYC-Online. 113.*

VanderVen, K. (2009). Why focusing on control backfires: A systems perspective. *Reclaiming Children and Youth. 17* (4). 8-12.

Vanderwoerd, J. (1991). Divisions between behaviour management and therapy: Towards new directions of authority in child and youth care. *Journal of Child and Youth Care. 5*(1), 33-41.

* * *

Originally published in *Relational Child and Youth Care Practice* (2013), Vol 26(2), pp 6-10

7

Sitting with Jason

Thom Garfat

I remember sitting beside Jason on the side of his bed. It was a small crowded room and the wall was right in front of us, no more than a foot or two away. As we sat there, every few minutes Jason would explode, lean forward and smash his fists in to the wall. We had been there a while and the wall was starting to look like a block of Swiss cheese, it had so many fresh holes in it. His fists, especially the knuckles, were starting to look like ground meat. But he was nowhere near stopping. He was following some internal rhythm of his own.

Jason's room was in the basement of his parent's home. Tiny and tucked away in the corner, but at least it was his – that's what he liked to say when he was feeling like talking, which wasn't often. Most of the time he just acted out his feelings, like he was doing now. Not always this dramatically, of course. Sometimes it was just a silent storming. Or a dark withdrawal from contact. Or disappearance.

I had tried everything I could think of over the past hour or so to bring him down, to help him regain control, to stop and move on from this intense rage he seemed to be experiencing. But nothing I had done, or was doing, made any difference. His rage just burned on. The only slowing was those moments between explosions when he seemed to simmer on high. I felt like I was sitting on the edge of a volcano and yes, I was nervous – okay, I was scared, too.

But I was also determined to hang in with him through this – whatever it was. And I sure didn't know what it was. Lorne had taught me that – hanging in even when you are unsure about what is going on. "Don't run fearfully from your own ignorance", he used to say.

I was there because that was what I did back then – visited young people in their homes and communities trying to help them find what I thought of as 'better ways'; better ways to live with others, better ways to live with themselves, better ways to get on with it. I was with Jason because he was messing up in school, had been arrested a few times and now was facing a sentencing hearing which, we all knew, was going to result in him being sent away for a while – to a 'school', as they were euphemistically called back then. We had been talking about the upcoming hearing – scheduled for the next day – when he started this explosive reaction. One minute we were talking, then there was a silence, and then the first explosion.

I call it a reaction because I thought he must be reacting to something. I had gone through all my own projections: that he was reacting to going away, that he realized how he had lead himself to this point, how he regretted what he had done... But none of that had connected with him and now I realized that was all about me. I had no idea what he was reacting to at all. I was lost. 'When you are lost, sit still' my grandpa used to say.

So, I was just sitting there. Doing nothing except being with him as he went through the cycle of explosions and simmering. Waiting. It didn't seem like there was much else to do. Well, really, it was just that I couldn't think of anything to do except leave or sit there. So there I sat.

And then I wondered if I should leave.

So I asked him, "Jason, would you prefer me to leave?"

He smashed the wall a few times: left, left, right, smash, smash. "No."

And that was it. Just 'No'. No 'do whatever you want'. No 'I don't care.' None of his customary responses. Just 'no'.

So I stayed.

Well, I won't drag it out here – let me just say it went on for some time. So I just sat there and after a while I seemed to enter into an almost trance like state – slightly disconnected and differently present – as if I was a little outside myself, or deeper in there.

And in that state it seemed to me that I could sense his rhythm. The swelling and receding. The rage and the simmer. The out and the in. After a while, I found myself leaning forward towards the wall at the exact moment he exploded in to it, and then leaning back as his strength was expended. As if I was connected somehow to whatever was going on in him. Connected in the experience.

Forward, smash, release, back. Forward, smash, release, back. A rhythm of pain and destruction. A dam building up pressure and then releasing, only to build up again.

And after a while, as simply as it started, it was done. One final release and then rest. Drained. Exhausted. Finished. Over.

Jason sat there for a minute and then said, "Thanks'. That was it. No explanation. No discussion. Just 'thanks' and then he got up quietly and left his room. I followed.

We walked upstairs to where his parents were sitting in the living room. I could see by the white drained faces turned towards us that they had been worried. The father looked to Jason and then to me. I had nothing to give him so he just waited.

Jason looked at his father and spoke. "I've ruined my wall again," he said. "I'd like to fix it before I go away tomorrow. Will you help me?"

Now Jason never asked for anything, never said he had done anything wrong and certainly never asked for help. His father looked momentarily stunned – but, I must confess, no more than I, for sure. His mother looked on, worried it seemed.

His father responded calmly, tentatively. "Sure, but it's not really necessary. I can do it."

I'd rather do it," Jason replied. "And I would like to do it now."

"No, really," his father said.

"Yes, really," Jason responded.

"Okay," his father answered. "I got the stuff in the basement. I'll go get it."

"I'll come with you," Jason said.

In case you are wondering, I was just standing there watching this go on. I had never seen Jason and his father do anything but fight – yell, stomp, hurt, retreat.

Jason's mother spoke up. "Let me fix your hands, Jason."

"Not right now, Mom. Maybe later."

"But you can't work on the wall with your hands like that."

"Oh, I think I can," he replied. Turning to his father, he asked, "Unless it bothers you, Dad?"

Now this was just getting to be too much. Not only was Jason not fighting with his father, and was asking him for help, but now he was checking out how he felt about something. I waited for his father to tell him to get cleaned up. That would have been the normal routine. Then the argument would start. But that didn't happen.

"But... " his mother started. "Its okay," his father interjected, looking at Jason.

"It's up to you, son."

"That's what you always say," Jason laughed lightly. "And then I usually make the wrong decision."

His father laughed back. "So true. Did it myself a number of times when I was your age. Still do. Let's go get started."

His mother looked on, amazed and hesitant I suspect about this different-than-usual exchange between father and son.

We went back downstairs to the other corner of the basement and into the workshop where his father seemed to retreat to so often. Jason's dad rumbled around for a few minutes and came up with some wall plaster powder, a trowel and some clothes. "We'll need some water," he said.

"I'll get it," Jason responded. And he did.

I was still there, just tagging along but I wanted to know where this was all going. And, truth is, I was waiting for it all to fall apart, or erupt into something crazy, or get back to 'normal'.

Once Jason had the water, he led the way and we all went in to his bedroom and surveyed the damage. The wall was a real wreck where he had been smashing it. I felt guilty, like I should have stopped him. It was as if my failure to be helpful was tattooed into the wall. I felt shame standing there.

Jason's dad must have sensed what I was feeling because he

turned to me and told me I could clean off the loose pieces while he and Jason mixed the plaster powder and water. I was glad to have something to do but as I moved to start the clean-up, Jason spoke.

"You didn't do it. I did. I'm going to clean it up myself."

"I think maybe he needs to do it, Jason," his father said, while I stood there wondering where this suddenly sensitive man had come from. "We can get the plaster ready while he does that."

Jason looked at his Dad and then at me, and then simply said 'okay'. So I started to clean up the edges of the holes. When I was finished Jason and his Dad were standing behind me with bucket, trowels, and mesh in hand. Waiting for their turn at the wall. I stepped aside.

"I'll do it," Jason said again, this time referring to making the actual repairs.

"Do you know how?" his Dad asked.

"Sure. You taught me years ago the first time I did this."

"And you remember?"

"I remember everything," Jason said.

"I never would have guessed," his father said. "You always seemed to ignore me. It was like I was talking to a brick wall."

'Ah, here it comes,' I thought.

"Ya, I know," was all Jason replied, reaching in to the bucket of mix to give it a stir.

So he set to work on the wall, scraping, putting the mesh in place, plastering the holes until finally they were all done. His father stood beside him.

When he was finished, we all sat on the bed together looking at the wet patches which were his work, waiting for it to dry enough for sanding. Earlier I had sat there looking at destruction happening. Now we sat there looking at reparation. It was like we had shifted to a different universe; like it was Act Two with different actors filling in.

"Well, fine job," Jason's Dad said. "But what were you thinking when you pounded all those wholes?"

"I was thinking that if I just kept it up long enough he," indicating me with a flick of his head, "would just go away and leave me alone. But he didn't."

"But you told me to stay," I said somewhat defensively, I must confess.

"No I didn't," Jason replied, shaking his head. "You asked if you should leave and I told you that I didn't care. That it was up to you. When you didn't leave, I thought that if you can get through this so can I."

Well, I wanted to argue with him about what I had said but then I thought 'what's the point?' What's important was what he heard, what he experienced, and what he made of it. Well, maybe that's what I think now. Back then I probably just didn't want to spoil the moment.

"Anyway, after a while, with you just sitting there, it all began to seem stupid. What I was doing I mean, pounding the wall. And then I realized my hands hurt. Hell, at one point I thought you were going to smash the wall with me the way you leaned forward when I did. So I thought one of us had to quit what we were doing."

Now, of course, I wanted to ask him what he was talking about, but I didn't.

"So, I stopped. And then I it was like I realized it was like I was always hurting myself. In all kinds of ways, not just my hands. And that seemed stupid too. So I decided to quit that too. It just all seems so stupid now."

Jason's father looked at me like I should have something to say, which I didn't, of course. Then he looked at Jason. "Stop what?" he asked.

"Everything," Jason said. All the stupid stuff I have been doing for years. I decided to stop it all. Now I just want to get it over with. So when I go to court tomorrow I am just going to do whatever the judge says and start over. It's time."

"Sounds good to me," his father said. And I have to confess I admired how he just let it go – the opportunity to say 'about time', or 'like I have always said', or something else provocative.

"Yup," Jason replied, staring at his work. "Looks like the wall is dry enough to sand. I'll do it."

"I'd like to help." his father said.

"Okay, we can do it together."

Then the father turned to me. "I don't know what you did, but thanks."

"He made me look at myself, that's what he did," Jason interjected. "He was always telling me I was stupid to hurt myself."

Now, I'm sure I never said that. I wouldn't have told him he was stupid. That would have ended our relationship for sure.

"God knows I've tried to do tell you that a few times myself," his father said. "But it never seemed to work. You always shut me out."

I waited. Anticipating.

Jason said something about how that was then and this is now and reached out to touch the wall. "Besides, this time he didn't say anything, so I couldn't argue with him."

"Well, I didn't know what to say," I replied. "But now I gotta go. See you tomorrow Jason."

"Don't come pick him up," his father said. "His mother and I will drive him to court tomorrow."

Turning to Jason, looking at him like he really was his son, he spoke. "I guess if you're gonna change, I guess we should too."

When I turned to leave, they were standing side by side, sanding the plaster over the holes. A different rhythm. A safer one it looked like to me. A healing one. Connected in a different experience.

And as I walked away from the house, I wondered what had happened. How had these two people moved from antagonism and hostility to cooperation? How had it all changed from a rhythm of destruction to a process of repair? God knows how it happened. I sure didn't.

***

Originally published in *Relational Child & Youth Care Practice*, 2006, Vol 19(1), pp. 53-56.

8

It's Only a Matter of Time: Cross-Cultural Reflections

Leon Fulcher

Whilst living and working in Europe, I once heard a story about an exchange between an American and a Scotsman that made me chuckle – since it echoed my own cross-cultural experiences with both parties, as shown it what follows:

A young American from that country's Southwest was touring the Highlands of Scotland. He found himself one evening in a traditional Highland pub where he engaged one of the locals in wide-ranging conversation about differences between their respective countries. Late in the conversation, the young American explained how, where he lived, there was a common phrase *"Mañana, Mañana"* which means "tomorrow, or by and by", the "mañana habit" being a Spanish-American phrase of procrastination. The young American asked his new Scottish friend if there was anything similar in the local vernacular. The Scotsman thought for a time before answering "I cannae think of a phrase that conveys such a state of urgency".

Having lived and worked internationally for more than thirty years in Europe, the South Pacific and the Middle East – with blocks of time spent also in Malaysia and China – the issue of time and its cross-cultural meanings has been a recurring theme underpinning all those experiences.

My first international trip came as an eye-opener since the only real encounter with time differences before that time involved crossing between Mountain and Pacific time zones as a youth travelling to visit my grandfather. Some personal reflections about cross-cultural meanings of time are offered in what follows in the hope they might be of interest since time impacts so directly on relational child and youth care practice. Drawn from personal and professional experience, attention is drawn to ten questions that highlight different themes about time and what textbooks call "tempocentric perspectives" that impact on child and youth care practice.

1. What Day Is It? – A focus on calendars

Most children and young people grow up learning to read a calendar but few learn that in different places, there are different calendars. In the West, young people grow up learning to read time according to a solar calendar based on the positioning of the earth as it revolves around the sun. Elsewhere many people learn to use a lunar calendar which calculates time according to the positioning of the moon. For example, December 2, 2005 (2/12/2005) in the solar calendar translates into November 1, 1426 (1/11/1426) in the Hijri or Islamic lunar calendar. The free encyclopedia website *Wikipedia* offers a treasure chest of information about cross-cultural variations when it comes to calendars. For example, one finds that the *Gregorian calendar* is used nearly everywhere in the world. A modification of the Julian calendar, it was first proposed by the Neapolitan doctor Aloysius Lilius, and was decreed by Pope Gregory XIII, for whom it was named on 24 February 1582. The *Julian calendar* was introduced in 46 BC by Julius Caesar and took force in 45 BC (709 *ab urbe condita*)[1]. It has a regular year of 365 days divided

---

1   *Ab urbe condita* (AUC or a.u.c.) is Latin for "from the founding of the city" (of Rome), supposed to have happened in 753 BC. It was one of several methods used for dating years in the Roman era, when the Roman calendar and the Julian calendar were in use. It appears to have been widely replaced

into 12 months, and a leap day is added to February every four years. Hence the Julian year is on average 365.25 days long. Those who care about such matters note that the astronomical solstices and the equinoxes advance, on average, by about 11 minutes per year against the Julian year, causing the calendar to gain a day about every 134 years, hence the argument given for changing to the Gregorian calendar, 50 years after Jacque Cartier discovered Canada and claimed it for France.

The Islamic calendar (also called "Hijri calendar") is the calendar used to date events in many predominantly Muslim countries. A purely lunar calendar having 12 lunar months in a year of about 354 days, this is used by Muslims everywhere to determine the proper day on which to celebrate Muslim holy days. Because this lunar year is about 11 days shorter than the solar year, Muslim holy days, although celebrated on fixed dates in their own calendar, usually shift 11 days earlier each successive solar year. Islamic years are also called Hijra years after the first year of the Prophet Muhammad's migration from Mecca to Medina. Thus each numbered year is designated either H or AH, the latter being the initials of the Latin anno Hegirae (in the year of the Hijra). Most lunar calendars are also lunisolar, such as the Hebrew, Chinese and Hindu calendars, as were most calendar systems used in antiquity. The reason for this is that a year is not evenly divisible by an exact number of lunations, so without any correction the seasons will drift with respect to the calendar year. The only widely-used purely lunar calendar is the Islamic calendar, which always consists of twelve lunations. As a result of this, it is mostly used for religious purposes, alongside a secular solar calendar, and Islamic feasts perform a full circle with respect to the seasons every 33 years.

If that isn't confusing enough, depending on one's cultural traditions or where one lives, one might use the Bahá'í calendar

by the anno Diocletiani (A.D.) system which in turn was gradually superseded by the anno Domini (A.D.) system of Dionysius Exiguus. Some have claimed that an era *ab urbe condita* (from the founding of the city of Rome) did not, in reality, exist in the ancient world, and the use of reckoning the years in this way is modern.

which has 19 months, each having 19 days, the Coptic calendar based on the ancient Egyptian calendar; the Iranian calendar – used widely in Afghanistan; or the Thai solar calendar which counts from the Buddhist era. It is also worth noting that indigenous peoples of North America, the South Pacific and elsewhere in South America and Africa operate with their own particular calendar variations. Given such a variety of calendars, one might reasonably ask what relevance this could possibly have for child and youth care practice? The answers depend on the extent of cultural diversity within any given group of children or young people and their families with whom one is working. The greater the diversity, the more important it may be to take account of possible differences in the way families calculate time. Perhaps more importantly, one must become ever wary about assuming that time is measured according to the "facts" that appear on one's own personal calendar and timepiece. How many different calendars might be influential when determining yearly plans at your work place?

2. What Season Is It? – A focus on climatic changes and human activity

A season is one of the major divisions of the year, generally based on periodic changes in weather over the course of a year – however measured. In the so-called temperate and polar regions of the world there are generally four seasons recognized as Spring, Summer, Autumn and Winter. But in the Southern Hemisphere, these seasons appear at different times of the solar year, such that one might comfortably wear shorts and t-shirt at Christmas time, and celebrate with a beach BBQ instead of being huddled beside a fire as in the Northern Hemisphere. In some tropical and subtropical regions it is quite common to speak of the rainy (wet or monsoon) season versus the dry season, as the amount of precipitation may vary more dramatically than the average temperature. In other tropical areas a three-way division into hot, rainy and cool seasons might be used. Then, in other parts of the world, special "seasons" are loosely defined according to natural events such as the hurricane or typhoon season, the tornado season, and a wild-fire or burning season. Still other places might identify the hunting season or the planting season, etc. The main point here is that time is once again divided into segments according to the climate, or by activities that are linked with climate. Child and youth care workers engaging with native youths in Northern Canada must plan their activities around traditional hunting, fishing and trapping seasons, when animals, birds and fishes move through migratory cycles and link time to seasonal activities for people. Elsewhere, child and youth care workers might find themselves engaging with young people according to particular sporting seasons, moving from football to basketball to ice hockey or baseball and cricket. In each example, human activities are linked to social activities, and time is measured from one season to the next – often without much conscious reflection given to what that might mean for kids and the families with whom we work.

3. What's The Time? – Greenwich Mean Time and Time Zones

Time zones represent another temporal dimension that will be instantly familiar to anyone who has travelled East or West for any distance at all. When driving, it is not uncommon to find signs posted to report a time zone crossing. Greenwich Mean Time (GMT) is the name given to mean solar time at the Royal Greenwich Observatory, Greenwich, London, England, which by convention is at 0 degrees geographic longitude. Noon Greenwich Mean Time is not the moment when the Sun crosses the Greenwich meridian (and reaches its highest point in the sky in Greenwich). Because of the Earth's uneven speed in its elliptic orbit and its axial tilt this event may be up to 16 minutes away from noon GMT but represents the annual average of the Sun's motion, thereby justifying the notion of 'mean' in Greenwich Mean Time. As Great Britain grew into an advanced maritime nation, English mariners kept their timepieces on GMT in order to calculate their longitude "from the Greenwich meridian". Such action did not affect shipboard time itself, which was still solar time. This combined with mariners from other nations using the same method, eventually led to GMT being used world-wide as a reference time independent of location. A scheme was devised where the surface of the planet was divided into twenty four "time zones", each separated by 15° of longitude and offset by one hour from its neighbour. And time zones have been identified as a number of hours and half-hours "ahead of GMT" or "behind GMT". Hourly time signals were first broadcast from Greenwich Observatory on 5 February 1924 and have continued ever since.

With the introduction of Daylight Savings Time in many parts of the world, one literally springs forward in time on a particular day and then leaps backward or returns to Standard Time roughly six months later in the year. Curiously, some places like the Province of Newfoundland in Canada have a half-hour time difference from everywhere else. Time zones feature prominently with international travel, especially if one crosses the International Date Line and loses or gains a whole day, depending on which direction one is flying. After such trips, one is almost always left with jet lag as the body clock reconfigures from one place and time zone to another. Child and youth care workers are often challenged to calculate the best time to make long distance telephone calls when supporting young people with family members living in other parts of the country. While time zones within a country may be mastered with relative ease, international telephone calls present greater challenges. Calls are not infrequently received in the middle of the night because a caller in one time zone has had difficulty working out 8 to 12-hour, or even 22-hour time zone differences. Child and youth care workers often don't have a moment to think about the impact of time zones. However, with increased travel and movements of family members to different parts of the country or world, it's not long before time zones become a reality in working relationships with kids.

4. What Day of the Week Is It? – Weekdays, Weeknights and Weekends

In practical terms, the working week for child and youth care is commonly divided into three important segments: weekdays, weeknights and weekends. For children and young people, weekdays are normally the time when they attend school, except during school holidays. For workers, weekdays are often about meetings and attending to issues for young people at times when the "professional" world is available. Weeknights on the other hand are commonly very active times in child and youth care work. Activities, clubs and outings are often built into weeknights, along with homework and quiet time, if ever there are such times. Weekends present even greater challenges and opportunities since these are the times when staff normally want time off work for family and social pursuits. Weekends are also times when young people make home visits, get involved in social activities with peers, and perhaps even get involved in activities that require interventions with authorities. Such patterns are fairly common in different parts of the world. However, few stop to consider that distinctions between weekday, weeknight and weekend actually change depending on cultural practices and where you live (Fulcher, 2002). For example, in the United Arab Emirates workdays run Saturday through Wednesday and the weekend is Thursday and Friday, with Friday being the holy day. In Israel, the weekend holy day of Shabot is Saturday, while elsewhere the weekend is Saturday and Sunday when Christians celebrate their holy day. Thus one finds that cross-cultural considerations play a big part in breaking time into segments called months, weeks and days. Child and youth care workers rarely have reason to stop and think about such matters unless cultural diversity in their programmes requires it. However, in very practical terms, try reorganising the staff roster to give added cover on the weekends and staff complaints will be heard complaining about needing time off with their families and friends. Or think about happens if the agency imposes an overtime ban. Such actions will quickly confirm that weekly time cycles do indeed matter, regardless of whether we stop to think about it.

5. What Do People Say About Time? – Daily Comments and Phrases

The story shared at the start of this paper referred to *"mañana"* as a Spanish-American phrase of procrastination. As one travels one finds that there are cross-cultural parallels almost everywhere. How many times might one hear North American kids say "later" when asked to complete their daily chores? Throughout the Middle East – in the Arabic world anyway – one frequently hears the phrase "*Inshaallah*" which literally means "if God wills it". Depending on how this word is used, it may actually refer to its literal meaning, as deeply religious people recognise that a higher power is required if they are to fulfil a given task. However, depending on the circumstances around which the phrase is used, "*Inshaallah*" may also mean something like "ok, if I get around to it". A related phrase adds a specific time dimension to such exchanges when one hears "*Bukra Inshaallah*". With such an alteration, the literal meaning becomes "tomorrow if God wills it". However, the cultural meaning is more likely to be something like "I'll see what I can do" but without much commitment towards following through. So depending on where child and youth care workers find themselves, important messages are conveyed about time, as noted earlier in a discussion about metaphors used daily in this field of work (Fulcher, 2004). Amidst the hustle and bustle of a busy day or working week child and youth care workers rarely stop and think about such matters even though their relational work with young people and families might be that much more effective.

6. Whose Time Shall We Follow? – Western Time and Others' Time

Not everyone is aware that there are different attitudes and cultural traditions concerning time. Time orientation, time structuring or planning, and time management actually have quite different meanings in different cultures (Leigh, 1998). Cross-cultural exchanges between New Zealand Maori and New Zealanders of European origin will invariably highlight questions about which 'time' each party is using when organising an event. The same is likely to be true with respect to exchanges between Pacific Island peoples and peoples of European origins. This is not meant to imply that one cultural group maintains a high degree of time orientation while the other group doesn't. Instead, it's about what variables are taken into account when determining the right time for an event to begin. For Maori and Pacific Island peoples, the issue frequently concerns the issue of readiness and preparedness while for Europeans the concern is more likely to be what the clock says and when the event was supposed to begin. Similar issues are encountered in the Arab world where one might be asked whether the ground rules that apply will be Western time or Arabic time. Again the issue appears to be more about social readiness to begin rather than an arbitrary reading of the clock. The arts and literature are filled with examples of cross-cultural dilemmas when reviewing ways in which Westerners engage with indigenous peoples in different parts of the world where clocks and timepieces hold different meanings for both groups. And yet experiences in Asia have taught me to be "on time" since time management there may be even more rigorous than in the West. For all these reasons, child and youth care workers might usefully review how young people with whom they are working manage their time, especially with curfews and getting to school on time.

7. Does Time Ever Stand Still? – Time Out

Next time you are watching a televised sporting event, count how many times the referee calls "time out", whether because one of the teams seeks a pause in the proceedings or because someone rules that a short-term pause is required. In child and youth care work, there are many occasions when "time out" may be called, and such events have considerable meaning for all parties involved. "Time out" may be called for troublesome behaviour, as when a young person loses control and needs time to regain composure. Such periods are usually part of an overall treatment plan and are timed to follow immediately on from a tantrum or episode of unruly behaviour. Staff members also take "time out". This might occur after a particularly difficult incident at work when they need to regain composure or recover from the fatigue of an all-night crisis. "Time out" might also mean a supervised walk for a young person living temporarily in a secure unit, when one-to-one time is considered important and going for a walk is deemed therapeutic. As one travels internationally, it is interesting the ways in which different turns of phrase might be used to highlight this "time out" dynamic (Lakhoff & Johnson, 1980). For example, in Australia one might hear about somebody going "walk-about", while in New Zealand there are occasions when someone might be "going bush". In each instance, the result means taking some time out from the normal routine and often spending time alone or with very few others. Time doesn't really stop in such instances but how time is used does change compared with how it is spent by others. "Time out" normally means that something isn't just right and there is need to get something sorted out before signalling "time in" and resuming play. In child and youth care, knowing when to call "time out" and use such time productively is an essential feature of good practice.

8. What's The Deadline? – Just in the Nick of Time

Each day there are deadlines that child and youth care workers have to meet. The school bus arriving, meals on the table, reports being written – all represent deadlines of one sort or another that need to be met. Such time pressures add greatly to the stresses associated with child and youth care work, and all the more so when different young people have urgent needs that have to be met – all at the same time! Child and youth care workers may have faced deadlines if they enrolled in college or university courses and were given precise timelines when course assignments had to be submitted. Deadlines are also faced whenever applying for a new job or promotion within the same agency. In each case, clear messages are given about when applications close or when paperwork must be handed in to be considered for a particular position or promotion. In reality, deadlines are a daily feature of this work. When responding to deadlines one is commonly faced with urgency, regardless of whether the 'urgent' matter is actually important. The more one deals with *urgent* matters the harder it is to refocus on the *important* matters that might really make a difference. So child and youth care workers need to ask: Is this engagement with a particular young person really urgent or important? Is it both urgent and important? Or do we need to refocus attention on what is important with this kid and let somebody else attend to what may seem urgent to somebody else? There are many ways in which the message "hurry up" is conveyed to many people in child and youth care work. How often do we "slow down" and pay greater attention to the little issues that are really important for kids?

9. What's Happening? – Now, Not Now and Immediacy

When child and youth care workers find themselves in the midst of a crisis, time takes on quite a different dimension associated with immediacy. It's not that time suddenly stands still; it's more about requiring one to focus on the meaning of "Now" and what is happening right now with this young person in this situation and place. Everything else fades into the background, especially when a child is sick, a wound is bleeding, a suicide attempt has been initiated, or when a fight has to be calmed.

In instances such as these, distinctions between "now" and "not now" are blurred by the immediacy of relational engagement. But crisis situations are not the only such instances when "now" and "not now" are important. When engaging with young people who have attention deficit problems, or autism, a child and youth care worker needs to maintain focus on immediacy since behavioural prompts and feedback are often the central issues for responsive work with such youngsters. There is often little time for reflection until after the immediate concerns in the encounter have moved on, and some elements of closure or new level of stability has been achieved. In such cases it is difficult to focus on deferred gratification or to plan very far ahead because of the particular time orientations that such young people present. Time issues like these can be encountered on a daily basis in some child and youth care situations. Without careful thought and attention to how workers respond on such occasions there are frequently missed opportunities and our professional interventions with young people become re-active instead of pro-active.

10. What Is Tempocentric Socialisation? – Vacations and School Holidays

Finally, it may be worthwhile stepping back from specific

questions to consider the wider issue associated with time orientations and how we acquire them. This is not to suggest that one start
using the technical term "tempocentric" in daily exchanges or in
child and youth care staff meetings. It is important, though, to recognize that the subject of this paper has been and is the subject of
international scholarly research, not simply personal reflections.
First of all, the word "tempo" is the Italian word meaning "time".
Those who have studied music or performed musically at any time
will know that "tempo" is linked to the idea of rhythms, and how
slow or fast a piece of music is played. "Centric" on the other hand
means "having or being situated at or near a center". Hence one
might find certain parallels between "egocentric", "ethnocentric"
and "tempocentric". Someone who is "tempocentric" tends to
identify their own personal and cultural interpretations of time as
absolute, or as being more important than any others. But how,
you might ask, does one develop a "tempocentric" perspective? As
one thinks back to their primary and secondary school experiences,
what memories come to mind? Did the school bell ring at set inter-
vals thereby reinforcing messages about time? Did school holidays
and vacation periods follow particular dates or correspond with
particular public holidays?

One acquires a particular time orientation through daily socialisation experiences and the sum total of these reinforce a particular
"tempocentric" perspective. Unless one engages in cross-cultural
experiences that take them out of their own particular time zone or
socio-cultural template, there is little reason to question whether
time is an absolute measure or a highly variable concept shaped directly by cultural meanings. So when asked "What time is it?" there
are actually quite a variety of answers that might be given, depending on who is asking and where they are directing their question.

Conclusion

In conclusion, ten questions have been asked and themes considered about meanings of time that often impact on child and
youth care practice. Whether referring to calendars, to seasons of
the year, contemplating time zones or days of the week,

conversational comments or cultural orientations about time, taking time out, meeting deadlines, responding to a crisis or reflecting on how one acquires a particular time orientation – each theme is arguably important if child and youth care practice is to be truly relational. Relational involves an attitude or stance which two or more persons or groups assume toward one another. As such it requires an aspect or quality that connects two or more things or parts as being or belonging or working together or as being of the same kind. Relational means the state of being mutually or reciprocally interested, and so long as one time orientation remains dominant and another's time orientation is ignored, misunderstood or rejected, then little progress can be made about working together towards shared aims. It is easy to say that "it's only a matter of time". But for someone operating from a different time zone', tempo or calendar, it is fundamentally important that one pays attention to their world, not just our own.

References

Fulcher, L C (2004) Learning Metaphors for Child and Youth Care Practice, *Journal of Relational Child and Youth Care Practice*. Volume 7, Number 2, pp. 19-27.

Fulcher, L C (2002) Cultural Safety and the Duty of Care, *Child Welfare*. Volume LXXXI, Number 5, pp. 689-708.

Lakhoff, G & Johnson, M (1980) *Metaphors We Live By*. London: The University of Chicago Press.

Leigh, J W (1998) *Communication for Cultural Competence*. Sydney: Allyn & Bacon.

* * *

An earlier version of this paper was published in *Relational Child & Youth Care Practice*, 2005, Vol 18 (4), pp. 58-64.

9

Daily Life Events in the context of CYC education

Kelly Shaw, Jeff Reid and Jacolyn Trites

The utilization of daily life events for therapeutic purposes is one of the cornerstones of a Child and Youth Care [CYC] approach to practice. Being in the moment engaged in the minutia of activities of daily living, mindfully and intentionally engaged in interaction with a youngster or family and using what comes up when it comes up is recognized (in part) as what makes a CYC approach unique from other forms or ways of helping (Garfat & Fulcher, 2012).

What might using daily life events look like in a post-secondary education program that supports the education of future CYC practitioners? Over the past few years facilitators of CYC education have been asking questions like this. At conferences we share stories of our experiences in the classroom and we have begun to write and publish about our practice – in this context.

As educators or facilitators of CYC education we (the authors) have spent time talking about our transition from practice with young people and families to our practice supporting CYC learners[1] and how many parallels to practice we experience. The

---

1   We prefer the term learner because it is defined as an individual who is

Canadian Child and Youth Care Educational Accreditation Board of Canada identifies that CYC is "a field of practice that includes front-line practice, supervision, management, *education*, and research (Outcomes Assessment Accreditation Model for Child and Youth Care Programs, n.d., p.4)." Thus, it stands to reason that discussion about the characteristics that are understood to be representative of CYC practice should be discussed as they might appear in these various contexts.

Curriculum that is based on recognized CYC competency documents[2] is the primary framework used to structure our education program to ensure that learners who reach graduation are prepared to enter the field of practice at a place of beginning readiness. Paralleling our beliefs about CYC practice, we meet each learner where they are at (in terms of experiences and professional development) when they enter the program, and engage with them supporting their move towards practice readiness. After a decade or more of supporting CYC learners we recognize that each learner is an individual and the approach we use and programming goals we develop with learners capitalize on individual strengths and areas of need.

While we know that students are not yet practicing CYC – they are learning about CYC theory and practice in an environment that parallels numerous characteristics of practice and thus are engaged in a developmental process that has not been clearly articulated. As faculty we use the stages of CYC worker development captured by Phelan (n.d.) and position ourselves as we would with beginning CYC workers. We support the creation of a safe environment recognizing that learners feel overwhelmed and often uncomfortable with the tasks that are asked of them, knowing full well that if

acquiring experience, ability or skill versus the term student that is defined as one who attends school (Merriam-Webster Dictionary, n.d).

2   For example: Competencies for Professional Child & Youth Work Practitioners (www.cyccb.org/storage/competencies_2010.pdf); Alberta CYCAA Certification Competencies (www.cycaa.com/certification/cycaa-certification); Ontario Child and Youth Worker Program Standard (www.tcu.gov.on.ca/pepg/audiences/colleges/progstan/humserv/echildyt.pdf)

learners are to engage in a learning (change) process they must feel safe in relationship and safe in environment.

Illustrating a Typical Learner

Logan[3] entered the second year of our program eager to engage in direct practice with young people. Her primary area of interest was community based practice. As often happens, she struggled to transition from her first year faculty supervisor to either of the faculty supervisors who were available for her in her second year. She identified that she had trust issues and continued to rely on her first year faculty as a support. As second year faculty supervisors, we began to hang out (spending time with intent and purpose) near her —in class, in the cafeteria, during structured and unstructured group work times. Our goal was to build trust and safety in relationship so that we could then begin to challenge some of the other behaviour that was showing up as potentially problematic. We connected often, as a team of faculty – as we would if we were working with a youth in a program (another parallel to practice). We identified that rapport and trust were beginning for her when she began to engage in a way that we interpreted as genuine and self-focused rather than behaviour that was reluctant, resistant, or attempts to please faculty. Once this was established, we began to gently identify how we interpreted her showing up and how others might interpret and experience her.

Logan was a young person – just three years out of high school. She wore baggy jeans and baggy sweaters. She had several facial piercings – perhaps what might have been called a grunge look. Based on our experiences we were confident young people would be attracted to her and she was eager and keen to engage with them, so this would clearly meet her needs. Our concern was that she had not yet developed her own self-awareness to a point that she would understand the needs of the youth in their desire to engage with her.

---

3   Logan is an alias. We have to the best of our memory never had an individual in our program named Logan.

Discussing choice of dress and presentation of one's individuality with learners is challenging, yet it is a concrete example of using daily life events for the benefit of the learner. Being willing to be confronted by our own experience of other in this dialogue is an example of our relational engagement with learners. Supporting Logan to identify why she chose the style of dress that she did; why she pierced her face, and how she was going to incorporate these choices into her use of self as she learned to therapeutically engage with youth, required us to use all of our CYC practice skills. Distinguishing our feelings about her wallet chain and our reaction to her baggy pants – the meaning we made of our experience of her – was essential in order to effectively support her to explore how she would be experienced by others given her choice of dress code. People form impressions based on first-time encounters and unless there are repeated contacts, there may be no opportunity to clarify first impressions. It was important that Logan understand that in CYC, relational practice is not just about on-going relationship development, it can be about the one encounter (Gharabaghi, 2010).

Preparing Learners

Preparing CYC practitioners in an educational environment is multifaceted and is ultimately about preparing individuals to practice in very demanding, contextually complex environments. Child and Youth Care practice is recognized as a unique way of helping children, youth, and families (Gharabaghi, 2010; Jones, 2007). Educating CYC practitioners requires a mixture of role-modeling, valuing the learners' struggles, supporting the development of their self-awareness and their relational skills, as well as skillfully delivering relevant theory (Phelan, 2005).

Phelan (2005) identified the importance of recognizing that CYC education is complex. Individuals who educate CYC practitioners need to be prepared to recognize the shift from working front line with young people to facilitating CYC education. Phelan suggests that this shift is significant and faculty need preparation, support, and a model of educational programming that is congruent with the needs of the learners in their process of development.

It is recognized that using daily life events in a caring way for the benefit of the young person or, in the case of this story, the CYC learner, requires that we have knowledge about the process of change (Garfat, 2002). Therefore, it is essential that facilitators of CYC education have a foundation for orchestrating activities that engage learners in challenging their skills and perceptions and developing their self-awareness. This is necessary so that facilitators are able to recognize areas of their own lives that require attention in order that they will be able to use self and the relationships they develop to support change in the youth with whom they engage.

Assessing the Learning and Change

It is has been our experience that learners in CYC education programs describe their experiences as transformational. At the end of her journey in the CYC program, Logan expressed having experienced learning more about herself than she could ever have imagined. It is our argument that using daily life events as a tool for this learning and subsequent transformation in an educational context is essential in a CYC education program. Transformation theory is grounded in the assumption that the way an individual learner interprets and reinterprets their experience in a culturally and contextually unique way is essential to their meaning making and therefore to their learning (Mezirow, 1997). Mezirow argues that "transformative learning is central to what adult education is all about (p. 226)".

Potentially one of the most challenging components of supporting the education and development of CYC practitioners is the element of assessment. We have incorporated a variety of assessment components that fall within an authentic assessment paradigm. The practice of authentic assessment is grounded in several assumptions: recognizing that the relationship between the teacher and the learner is important, that the learner is central to the process of learning, because learning is continuous, and that carefully considered assessment supports learning (Swaffield, 2011). It is recognized that in order to practice authentic assessment there has to be engagement between the parties involved in the assessment in order that the learner's context and voice are taken into consideration (Frey & Schmitt, 2007; Meyers & Nulty, 2009; Wiggins, 1993). Authentic assessment operates from a belief in the social construction of knowledge (John-Steiner & Mahn, 1996).

To be congruent with our knowledge of CYC practice, feedback to the learner and the assessment of the learner's skills has to be immediate (meaning making in the moment) and focused on the on-going skill development, while challenging the learner to undertake genuine self-assessment. As facilitators, we have incorporated video-taping of role-plays, using these opportunities to engage the learner in discussions about which interventions were used, the intent behind the intervention, and to assess the effectiveness of the intervention. The use of video removes the element of selective recall, and allows the learner to observe themselves as others may have perceived them. We use project based service learning; partnering groups of learners with community groups implementing projects that require them to directly engage with young people, and we supervise these projects as a faculty team. This gives us an opportunity to engage in supportive supervision using daily life events to support the understanding and incorporation of theory in practice.

For example, during one activity afternoon with a group of youngsters the CYC learners were having a hard time keeping the youngsters in the space that had been provided for them and focusing the youngsters on the activity they were facilitating. Faculty intervened and shut the door to the space – briefly highlighting space manipulation as it may benefit a youngster's feeling of containment (Feature, n.d.) and following up on the situation during the after program debrief. Being present with learners in the environment offers faculty the opportunity to use daily life events to support learning and development not unlike a supervisor would with a new worker (Michael, 2007).

The Complexity

It is difficult to discuss the utilization of daily life events without merging with other characteristics that are recognized as foundational to a CYC approach to practice. We have attempted to highlight how we use daily life events and to articulate how daily life is framed in our facilitation of CYC education within a pedagogical framework. While using daily life events for the benefit of others directs one to the minutia of everyday life, as Maier (1987) captured it – it is much more complicated than it appears. It is subtle and gentle and to the individual watching unaware, it may seem like nothing at all has transpired. What is clear to us is that we have further exemplified the complexity of CYC practice that has been written about by others (e.g., Garfat, 2003; Gharabaghi, 2009; Phelan, 2008; Ricks, 2001). As it continues to evolve, educators of future CYC practitioners need to articulate their pedagogy, and continue to synthesize the theoretical base that supports learning for child and youth care practice.

References

Outcomes Assessment Accreditation Model for Child and Youth Care Programs (n.d.). Retrieved from:
http://cyceduaccred.pbworks.com/w/file/fetch/62169862/Outcomes%20Assessment%20Model%20Dec%202012.pdf

Feature: Containment. (n.d.). The International Child and Youth Care Network [CYC-Net]. Retrieved from:
http://www.cyc-net.org/features/ft-containment.html

Frey, B. B., & Schmitt, V. L. (2007). Coming to terms with classroom assessment. *Journal of Advanced Academics*, 18(3), 402-423.

Garfat, T. (2002). The use of everyday events in child and youth care work. *CYC-Online.* Retrieved from:
http://www.cyc-net.org/cyc-online/cycol-0402-garfat.html

Garfat, T. (2003). Four parts magic: The anatomy of a child and youth care intervention. *CYC-Online.* Retrieved from:
http://www.cyc-net.org/cyc-online/cycol-0303-thom.html

Garfat, T. & Fulcher, L. C. (2012) Characteristics of a Relational Child and Youth Care Approach. *In T. Garfat & L. C. Fulcher (Eds) Child and Youth Care in Practice.* Cape Town: Pretext Publishing, pp. 5-24.

Gharabaghi, K. (2009). Too complicated, too fast. *CYC-Online.* Retrieved from:
http://www.cyc-net.org/cyc-online/cyconline-oct2009-gharabaghi.html

Gharabaghi, K. (2010). *Professional issues in child and youth care practice.* London: Routledge.

John-Steiner, V., & Mahn, H. (1996). Sociocultural approaches to learning and development: A Vygotskian framework. *Educational Psychologist, 31*(3/4), 191-206.

Jones, L. (2007). Articulating a child and youth care approach to family work. *CYC-Online*. Retrieved from http://www.cyc-net.org/cyc-online/cycol-0709-jones.html

Learner - Definition and More from the Free Merriam-Webster Dictionary. (n.d.). In *Dictionary and Thesaurus* - Merriam-Webster Online. Retrieved from http://www.merriam-webster.com/dictionary/learner

Maier, H. (1987). *Developmental group care of children and youth: Concepts and practice*. New York: Haworth Press.

Meyers, N. M., & Nulty, D. D. (2009). How to use (Five) curriculum design principles to align authentic learning environments, assessment, students' approaches to thinking and learning outcomes. *Assessment & Evaluation in Higher Education, 34*(5), 565-577.

Mezirow, J. (1997). Transformative learning: Theory to practice. *New Directions for Adult & Continuing Education*, (74), 5.

Michael, J. (2007). Some characteristics of a child and youth care approach as they apply to life space supervision. *CYC-Online*. Retrieved from http://www.cyc-net.org/cyc-online/cycol-0307-michael.html

Phelan, J. (n.d.). Stages of child and youth care worker development. *CYC-Online*. Retrieved from http://www.cyc-net.org/phelanstages.html

Phelan, J. (2005). Child and youth care education: The creation of articulate practitioners. *Child & Youth Care Forum, 34*(5), 347-355. doi:10.1007/s10566-005-5907-4

Phelan, J. (2008). Living with complexity and simplicity. *CYC-Online*. Retrieved from: http://www.cyc-net.org/cyc-online/cycol-0308-phelan.html

Ricks, F. (2001). Challenges be damn or changed? (Complexity in the practice process). CYC-Online. Retrieved from: http://www.cyc-net.org/cyc-online/cycol-0301-ricks.html

Student - Definition and More from the Free Merriam-Webster Dictionary. (n.d.). In Dictionary and Thesaurus - Merriam-Webster Online. Retrieved from http://www.merriam-webster.com/dictionary/student

Swaffield, S. (2011). Getting to the heart of authentic assessment for learning. *Assessment in Education: Principles, Policy & Practice, 18*(4), 433-449.

Wiggins, G. (1993). *Assessing student performance*. San Francisco, CA: Jossey-Bass.

* * *

Originally published in *Relational Child and Youth Care Practice*, 2013, Vol 26(2), pp 43-47

10

The Use of Daily Life Events and an Ericksonian Utilisation Approach

Werner van der Westhuizen

Milton H. Erickson (1901-1980) was one of the most influential psychotherapists of his time. He practiced as a hypnotherapist and family therapist and his approach challenged much of the mainstream psychology and psychiatry of his era. Working on the edge of what was considered acceptable during his time, he developed a unique approach that depended greatly on the flexibility of the therapist, the cooperation of his clients, and the utilization of whatever the client brought into the therapeutic encounter. Erickson's practice as a psychiatrist displayed significant similarity to many characteristics of a child and youth care approach. His ideas and methods, therefore, can complement the skill set of the child and youth care practitioner. Erickson's approach was more developmental and strength-based than one would imagine from a medical psychiatric perspective and this helps to explain why he was so unpopular with the psychiatric community.

110

Similarities between child and youth care and a utilization approach

Garfat and Fulcher (2012) describe the characteristics of a child and youth care approach to working with children and young people, which evolved over time into a distinct method of practice. It is therefore interesting to note the similarities between these basic principles of child and youth care and Erickson's utilization approach, which developed primarily from a psychiatric practice. For example, Erickson believed in utilizing the environment and behaviour of his clients to the extent that he designed social encounters in order to provide them with a therapeutic experience. In a keynote address by Jay Haley at the Fifth International Congress on Ericksonian Approaches, Haley recounts how Erickson typically made use of "auxiliary personnel" (Zeig, 1994). He would involve hairdressers, dressmakers, elevator operators, and children to design therapeutic encounters, something completely contrary to the mainstream psychological thought of his time. Similarly, when child and youth care practitioners use *daily life events to facilitate change*[1], they use everyday moments in their interactions with children to help them find different ways of being in the world (Garfat, Fulcher & Digney, 2012). This powerful way of working takes full advantage of the relational nature of the child and youth care practitioner's interactions with children. It is flexible and adaptive, requiring the child and youth care practitioner to respond *in the moment*, without necessarily being able to predict or anticipate the child's behaviour or the environment's response. Erickson knew that anything can become a therapeutic opportunity if properly utilized and he worked with *intentionality* in creating a therapeutic milieu where his patients had the best chance of success.

Erickson believed it was important for a therapist to be personally involved with a client. He did not accept that a therapist

---

1   The characteristics of a child and youth care approach are italicized throughout this article, for emphasis.

should be like a blank screen or a neutral observer, as was the mainstream thinking at the time. It was his personal involvement that often allowed his clients to make the changes they wanted (Gilligan, 1987). This corresponds with Gannon's principle of *"engaging with the other person in a deep and profound manner"* (as quoted in Garfat & Fulcher, 2012, p. 8) that will impact both the practitioner and the young person. Despite being physically weakened by polio, Erickson frequently left the office to visit his clients, something unacceptable in his time. He did not believe that therapy was office-bound and so he entered the world of his clients, their life space so to speak: in those moments and spaces he did his work. He *worked in the now* – believing that single session therapy was not only possible but desirable and never argued that long-term therapy was better or "deeper". He clearly believed in the power of a single encounter; that a moment could be all that was needed to make a significant change.

Child and youth care practitioners purposefully seek out the *strengths* in children and families in order build on these in their interactions. This focus enables children to experience themselves as competent and worthy (Garfat & Fulcher, 2012) and is often the beginning of positive changes for children. Erickson strongly believed that each person is unique and he showed an appreciation for the diversity of his clients, working to help them utilize their own circumstances as the basis for self-development (Gilligan, 1987). He assumed that people have far more abilities and resources than they are consciously aware of and never attempted to add anything to the client, but rather to assist the client in learning to utilize the skills and resources they already have.

Considering insight-oriented interpretations to be rude, Erickson was instead rather courteous and fully entered the world of the client before he considered how he could facilitate change. He accepted the client's reality to be a metaphor which could be utilized to communicate an idea to the client, rather than being something to be corrected. He preferred to *meet people where they are at,* accepting them for how they are and who they are. He conducted his therapy having fully accepted the world and the reality of his client and rather than confront or correct the client's problem, he utilized whatever the client offered him. Similarly, Krueger states that child and youth care practitioners place a high value on being able to enter the world of the client and meeting them on their own ground (Garfat, Fulcher & Digney, 2012).

While Erickson avoided making interpretations, he attached a critical importance *to meaning making*. According to Garfat (2004) meaning making is the process a person goes through in making sense of their experiences. For Erickson, those experiences were absolutely critical and were very much what his therapy was centred on. Zeig (1994) states that change is not only about the information we receive, but the *experiences we live*. While people may understand something in an intellectual sense by possessing the knowledge, it is only through their experiences that they can make meaning of that knowledge. Erickson was an expert at providing his clients with such experiences. Essentially, he would accept what the client brought to the encounter with him, enter the client's world, and provide the client with an experience that made sense in the client's own reality: a significant memorable encounter. Erickson would provide this encounter in a special way that would have meaning for his client, something that Zeig calls "gift-wrapping" the experience for the client. In this way, Erickson was purposeful and *intentional* in every interaction with his clients, a characteristic that is valued by Molepo (Garfat & Fulcher, 2012) in child and youth care practice. Intentionality in child and youth care practice does not mean that spontaneity is abandoned, but rather that the practitioner reflects on his or her intentions and interactions.

Erickson's utilization approach was further developed after his death by Ernest Rossi, who studied and collaborated with Erickson for many years. Rossi (1993) developed his approach to mind-body communication and although this is essentially a hypnotherapeutic approach, Rossi does not make use of "suggestion" or "influential communication" in the conventional sense. Rossi's approach involves accessing state-dependent memory, learning and behaviour systems, and making the encoded information available for problem solving. The role of the therapist is that of a guide and facilitator. A key concept of this approach is Rossi's postulation that memory is a dynamic and constructive process whereby people synthesize a new subjective experience every time a past event is recalled. From this perspective, memory is not seen as static, objective information that can simply be retrieved, since it involves a process of constructing the memory every time it is retrieved. The opportunity presented by this approach is that each time we access the state-dependent learning, memory, and behaviour that encode a "problem", we have the opportunity to re-associate, reframe, and reorganize – the problem in a manner to resolve it (Rossi, 1993). This opportunity exists because the natural mind tends to repeat the same story with variations, constantly updating and reframing "reality" in order to keep up with the new information in the environment.

From this psychobiological approach, problems are seen as pathways and symptoms are seen as signals. Problems are considered to be the path to a person's growing edge and symptoms are signals of the need for personal development. As an approach that is essentially problem-centred, the practitioner uses the client's own words as far as possible because the language that encodes the problem is also the pathway to resolve it. The same creative mental process that was used to create the problem can be used to "un-create" it. In working with clients, Rossi's main strategy for the practitioner is to access and reframe the problem by striving to help clients; (1) recognise their symptoms as important mind-body signals and, (2) utilize their problems as opportunities to explore and actualise their creative resources. Symptoms are then converted into signals and problems are reframed as creative resources. The approach is to receive the symptom-signal and then facilitate a creative process of information transduction that may transform the negative aspects of the symptom into therapeutic responses (Rossi, 1993).

Utilization in child and youth care practice

As the focus shifts from a comparison of core characteristic to the practice of utilization, we explore how a practitioner may respond differently when using a utilization approach when responding to a client who is emotionally excited. At the start of the encounter a client may be anxious, depressed, angry, or experience some other sense of discomfort. The typical reaction of most helping professionals would be to apply techniques aimed at reducing the discomfort through relaxation or some other method to "calm down" the client. Most practitioners would argue that before a therapeutic conversation can take place, the client needs to be comfortable, contained, and calm. However, if we consider those "symptoms" to be signals, then calming down the signals is equal to killing the messenger. Anxiety, tension, stress, and symptoms at the beginning of an encounter may be natural signals indicating a readiness to perform important therapeutic work. This "readiness energy" (Rossi, 1993) needs to be utilized to motivate the therapeutic work and not suppressed with placating and reassurances. Furthermore, Rossi (1993) also pays close attention to natural rhythms when a client spontaneously enters a quiet or inner-directed mood and utilizes these for the client to do "inner work". While in the context of Rossi's work he utilizes rhythms for hypnotherapeutic interventions, the important consideration is that he does not expect a client to respond to his interventions or his timing, but he respects the natural rhythm of the client and times his interventions accordingly. In the context of a child and youth care approach, Krueger refers to *rhythmicity* as a synchronized, dynamic connection between a practitioner and client (Garfat & Fulcher, 2012) where the emphasis is more specifically on the timing of the *interaction*. Although Rossi and Krueger may be referring to rhythms in somewhat different ways, the important note for the practitioner is that rhythms appear both intra-personally and interpersonally and that taking note of these rhythms allows the practitioner to time his or her therapeutic interactions in a purposeful and intentional manner.

This approach whereby there is a focus on the presenting behaviour seems to be a paradoxical intervention of prescribing the symptom, but from the psychobiological point of view it is not paradoxical at all. From this approach, to prescribe the symptom (even for a little while) is actually the most direct path to accessing the resources in the state-dependent memory, learning, and behaviour (Rossi, 1993). A paradoxical approach only seems paradoxical from the logical point of view wherein clients try to avoid the experience and expression of a problem in the hope that it will "go away". However, avoiding, resisting, or blocking the problem only prevents one from accessing and therapeutically reframing it.

While it must be acknowledged that Erickson and Rossi worked in the context of a traditional therapeutic office, a utilization approach lends itself easily to application in the child's natural environment. In fact, the active and creative imagination of children and young people make them very responsive to this approach. Instead of having counselling and therapy imposed from the outside, this approach allows the child to access their intuitive knowledge and utilize their natural resources. Given that child and youth care practitioners already work within the life space of the child, it provides them with a unique opportunity to implement utilization strategies and skills. While many interventions still focus on controlling and structuring the child's environment (outer world) in attempts to gain compliance with imposed structures, a utilization approach can provide a way to access and make the most of inner resources, an arena where each child is the expert of his or her own inner world. One of the benefits of incorporating ideas from the utilization approach into a child and youth care approach is that it naturally complements the existing skill set of the child and youth care practitioner, providing more ways of working with the inner world of the child.

Conclusion

The similarities between these two approaches warrant further exploration by the practitioner who may be interested in discovering how utilization strategies can enhance his or her existing skill set. Of course, any interventions must be contextually appropriate. One should also only practice skills and methods that one has been trained in, or in a setting where there is adequate supervision and support to try new skills and strategies. Most importantly, since all children and young people are unique, some will respond better to some approaches than others and it is ultimately a judgement call the practitioner makes to fit the approach to the child and not the other way around.

It seems fitting to conclude with one of Erickson's teaching tales that seemed "innocent" enough, but always had a profound meaning that would catch up with the listener at the right time. This is one of the stories he told about *thinking like children*:

> *"My youngest daughter went through college in three years, got a master's in her fourth year of college, and completed medical school in two years and nine months. When she was very young she would draw pictures and she'd remark as she was drawing: 'Drawing this picture is hard. I hope I get it done so I'll know what I'm drawing'"* (Rosen, 1982).

References

Garfat, T. & Fulcher, L. (Eds.) (2012). *Child and youth care in practice.* Cape Town: Pretext Publishers

Garfat, T., Fulcher, L. & Digney, J. (Eds.) (2012). *Readings for the therapeutic use of daily life events.* South Africa: Pretext Publishing

Garfat, T. (2004). Meaning-making and intervention in child and youth care practice. *Scottish Journal of Residential Care, 3,* (1), 113-124

Gilligan, S. G. (1987). *Therapeutic trances. The cooperation principle in Ericksonian Hypnotherapy.* New York: Brunner/Mazel Publishers

Rosen, S. (1982). *My voice will go with you. The teaching tales of Milton H. Erickson.* New York: W.W. Norton & Company

Rossi, E. L. (1993). *The psychobiology of mind-body healing. New concepts of therapeutic hypnosis (Revised Edition).* New York: W.W. Norton & Company, Inc.

Zeig, J. K. (1994). *Ericksonian Methods. The essence of the story.* New York: Brunner/Mazel Publishers

***

Originally published in *Relational Child and Youth Care Practice* (2013), Vol 26(2), pp 58-62.

11

Becoming Present: the use of Daily Life Events in Family Work

Kiaras Gharabaghi

Increasingly, services to address the challenges faced by families are moving from out-of-home settings to in-home settings, and child and youth care practitioners are being called upon to provide in-home interventions and support in multiple contexts. In the child welfare sector, for example, such work is often referred to as family preservation work, and is driven by the hope that such work will reduce the need for placing young people in foster or residential care. In the children's mental health sector, in-home support services are sometimes referred to as intensive family support programs and feature child and youth care practitioners who implement evidence-based models of intervention such as solution-focused therapies, collaborative problem solving or dialectical behavioural therapies. As these kinds of programs and services have proliferated and have accumulated much on-the-job learning, service providers have made several important observations (Al et al., 2012; Hurley et al., 2012; Kauffman, 2007; Tyuse, Hong, & Stretch, 2010), including:

- The challenges faced by families often cannot be neatly separated into 'clinical' or mental health challenges impacting a young person within the family on the one hand, and everyday challenges such as poverty, a lack of transportation, or general disorganization on the other hand. More commonly, families are challenged by the everyday experience of multiple issues, including seemingly trivial issues related to basic household management.

- Families are most appreciative of the relationship they develop with practitioners, and have relatively little interest in the specific model of intervention provided by the practitioner.
- Practitioners are almost always facing excessive caseloads, and are therefore unable to follow through on the relationship expectations of every family they are paired with; indeed, it is not uncommon for in-home support programs of any kind and in any sector to load practitioners up with twenty or more families.

These observations are important and should impact the way in which one approaches in-home support for families. From a child and youth care perspective, and especially in the context of the profession's commitment to a focus on daily life events, these observations challenge the practitioner's capacity to be/become present with families in ways that speak to the family's everyday experience of family conflict, problems, and dysfunction. The term 'presence' in this context has two distinct but related meanings. On the one hand, we can think of 'presence' in a physical or material sense whereby 'being present' denotes the practitioner's physical presence in the home. On the other hand, we can also think of 'presence' in its relational context, whereby 'becoming present' denotes the ever-evolving dynamics of those spaces (material and metaphorical) where the sensations of connectedness and mutual interdependence are strongly felt by both the family and the practitioner.

In the context of the three afore-mentioned observations about family work, the specific challenge to the practitioners is threefold:

- there is not a mandate to *be present* where one's presence is needed (e.g. the separation of clinical and everyday challenges);
- there is not enough opportunity to co-create with families a mutual understanding of what constitutes *becoming present* in their everyday lives (e.g. the feedback from families that it is all about relationships); and
- there is not enough time to *either be or become fully present* (e.g. the excessive caseloads of practitioners).

Overcoming these challenges requires an approach to exploring the concept of *becoming present* that integrates daily life events not with the concept of intervention (as it typically does in packaged family support programs) but instead with relationship (as is reflective of the core of child and youth care practice). This exploration must start with a reflection on the nature and role of relationships in the lives of families.

Relationships Beyond Interaction

In any relational context, the substantive impact of relationships unfolds far more so when we are physically apart than when we are physically together. Relationships are founded on the feeling of connectivity rather than the material context of coming together. Bellefeuille and Jamieson articulate the foundation for this idea: "relational practice is a dynamic, rich, flexible and continually evolving process of co-constructed inquiry" (as cited in Garfat & Fulcher, 2012). In residential child and youth care practice, for example, child and youth workers see themselves as 'having' relationships with the residents because they are having face to face interactions with the residents every day. When young people are asked about their experience while living in residential care, however, they typically cite their relationship with one or two of the staff as having been of great importance; somehow, the relationships with other staff members wither away and appear to have little sustainable impact on the young people. The most meaningful relationships are those that are 'present' (i.e. are felt) even when the parties to the relationship are apart. This kind of relational presence, manifested by the physical separation, can never just *be*, but most always *becomes*, reflecting the ever-evolving, never static nature of relationships.

In the context of in-home family work, then, working within relationship does not merely mean 'getting along well' while the practitioner is in the home. Instead, it means *becoming present* in the daily life of the family specifically when one is absent. This idea of 'being present' can easily be confused with the capacity-building context of packaged in-home support programs. There, the goal is to use one's physical presence (and one's interactions) in the home as a way of building capacity for a family to function differently in the practitioner's absence by essentially training the family to develop self-management skills. The fundamental goal is to render the relationship based on one's presence unimportant over time (i.e., becoming *absent*), so that the family can manage its challenges without that relationship by developing the skills necessary to overcome the challenges embedded in daily life events (McWey, Humphreys, & Pazdera, 2011). When we move relationships beyond the simple face-to-face interactions, the relationship becomes embedded in the experience of everyday family life and thus continues to be a substantive agent of change (and strength) for the family beyond those face-to-face interactions. The presence of the practitioner is felt in the context of the relationship rather than the material context of in-home intervention.

Finding Presence in Daily Life Events

Daily life events may include *activities* that unfold every day as well as *experiences* that capture the everyday unfolding of events and routines (Garfat & Fulcher, 2012). Activities might include waking up in the morning, meal times, recreational activities, doing homework, or getting ready for bed. Experiences might include feeling overwhelmed by the demands of the daily schedule, anger and frustration when things don't work out as expected or allowing relationships such as the spousal relationship between parents to be experienced as conflictual or burdensome. While there are obvious connections between activities and experiences in terms of daily life events, it is also important to note that such events may be experienced very differently by different members of the family.

In most family intervention programs, the goal is to help all members of the family to experience daily life events in harmonious ways, ensuring that conflict is avoided by proactively shaping daily life events to reflect the needs of everyone and to avoid features that are particularly challenging to one or some members of the family. Traditionally, this work was done by talking with family members about their everyday experiences, and then developing strategies to manage these experiences differently. The practitioner's role was to review the experiences of the family during each 'session' and to adjust the strategy based on what worked and what did not work.

Child and youth care approaches to family work change the method of family work by talking less and actually participating in the daily life events whenever possible: "The work is less reliant on dialogue and therapeutic reflection and more on experiential, lived moments, often co-experienced by the family and the worker" (Phelan, 2004; also Garfat, 2004; Shaw & Garfat, 2004). In other words, the child and youth care approach seeks a deeper understanding of how things are unfolding in a family and challenges family members to reflect on why they are unfolding in this way right then and there. This highlights the 'being in the moment' principle of child and youth care practice (Ward, 1998), and it helps to render the intervention less removed and abstract. Moreover, this approach to family work helps to re- frame family work as a joint project of the family and the practitioner, rather than the more traditional expert-driven frame- work that was common in typical in-home support programs.

Nevertheless, even this 'child and youth care approach to working with families' relies very substantially on the physical presence of the practitioner in the home of the family. The approach is not focused on daily life events *per se*, but instead on those daily life events that are experienced jointly by the practitioner and the family when the practitioner is in the home. As much as this approach seeks to do away with the office-based or session-based approach of earlier versions of family work, it is still one that relies substantially on physically coming together, replacing the office with the family home or any other setting where the family lives its life:

> *CYC practice is not oriented around temporally spaced and infrequent visits to an office where the client meets a therapist who has no experience of that individual's everyday life. Rather it is based on being in-the-moment with the individual(s), experiencing with them their life and living as it unfolds...* (Garfat & Fulcher, 2011, p.8).

Becoming present in family work takes this approach one step further and is specifically focused on embedding the relationship between the family and the practitioner in daily life events when the practitioner is absent. In other words, the goal of the practitioner is to seek out opportunities for presence through relationship rather than through interaction. As the family moves through its daily routines, including everyday events such as gathering for breakfast, doing homework, watching TV together or going shopping, the practitioner's presence is felt through his or her involvement, however nuanced, in these events, even when she is not 'physically present'.

By way of examples, we can imagine a practitioner preparing a particular recipe for the family dinner and leaving a shopping list for that recipe, so that when the family goes shopping, the practitioner becomes present as the required items are purchased. The practitioner may recommend a particular movie or TV show for the family to watch, so that when the family sits down to watch the show, the practitioner becomes present by having left his or her impressions of the show with the family to compare or contrast to the family's perspectives. Other creative ways of becoming present while absent include the introduction of competitions, such as board or card games, with every member of the family having to play each other as well as the practitioner, similar to a sports league. While the practitioner may only be able to play his or her games while physically present in the home, other family members can play each other within the context of the league in which the practitioner is one member. The outcomes of the games in his or her absence thus impact the standings of the league, and therefore cement the practitioner's presence even when he or she is not physically in the home. This concept of becoming present (and having an integral role) within the activity even when the practitioner is physically absent thus distinguishes this initiative from the more traditional 'homework assignments' common in more traditional family therapy approaches.

The presence of the practitioner can also be enriched through material contributions to the family[1]. For example, gifting the family a juicer, complete with a series of the practitioner's favourite shake recipes named after the practitioner and the individual members of the family (for example, the Kiaras Special, the Jack Terminator, or the Daddy Spectacular) results in new family customs and routines that speak to the relationship with the practitioner. Similarly, an evolving photo collage based on photos taken when the practitioner is physically present with the family and displayed prominently in the living room can provide a material reference point for the relationship between the family and the practitioner. This provides a daily reminder of that relationship and a talking point when the family is hosting friends or relatives.

Given the rise of new technologies, and in particular social networking media, additional opportunities for becoming present are available (Martin & Stuart, 2011). It is, for example, entirely possible to set up a Facebook page specifically for the family and the practitioner, that can serve to communicate and share daily life experiences between the family and the practitioner, as well as to post photos and ideas or recommendations for additional activities that might be of interest to the family. In this way, checking any updates to the page can become a daily routine for family members, again connecting the family to the practitioner and helping to enrich the relationship between the family and the practitioner.

1   I am drawing here on the ideas of Henry Maier (1987) with respect to 'transitional objects', although the context is quite different.

Similar opportunities exist in relation to tweeting, texting, or other social media technologies.

Family Enrichment through Daily Life Events

For many families, daily life events are experienced as problems and as obstacles to experiencing the 'good life'. The expectation of power struggles, physical confrontations, and verbal assaults often create enormous anxiety in approaching daily routines. What is more, in families that have for some time experienced difficulties related to daily life events, a sense of having to face these alone and bearing full responsibility for these can become overwhelming.

From a child and youth care perspective, on the other hand, it is precisely the daily life events, the everyday routines, and the seemingly trivial interactions that accompany these that present opportunities for positive and rewarding experiences (Garfat & Fulcher, 2012; Maier, 1987). From wake-ups to morning meals and from homework completion to recreational activities, the possibilities of joint experiences working to cement relationships and collective memories are limitless. Becoming present in family work, therefore, is fundamentally about re-constructing the anticipation associated with daily life events rather than their replacement with alternative routines.

The goal is to change the experience of daily life events from burdensome to enriching. This goal cannot be achieved through a process of 'intervention' alone. Instead, it can only be achieved by directly responding to the sense of overwhelming responsibility and ownership over managing these events felt by both parents and young people. Becoming present in family work is about the intentional use of relationship as a way of unburdening families from this overwhelming sense of responsibility and ownership pursuant to daily life events. The family and each of its members experience their daily lives in the presence of the relationship with the practitioner, instead of alone with the anticipation of being able to (or the burden of feeling one has to) report to the practitioner the next time he or she is physically present in the home.

In this sense, the focus on becoming present (in one's absence) changes the conceptual nature of 'relationship' in family work. Instead of 'relationship' being constructed as a contextual feature of family intervention work, or alternatively as a starting point for family intervention work, 'relationship' *becomes the intervention* (Stuart, 2009, p.222) that is dynamically contributing to the family's experiences of daily life events. Ultimately, change and growth within families unfolds within their life-space. Practitioners engaged in family support work must find ways of becoming present within this life-space, which cannot be limited to their physical presence; much like the life-space itself is not an entirely physical construct (Gharabaghi & Stuart, 2013). The use of daily life events provides an opportunity for transcending the concept of relationship as a material construct (e.g., *having* a relationship) and re-creating it instead as the relational practice of co-creating and co-experiencing "the space between us" (Garfat, 2008). But it does so most effectively when we become present in our absence.

References

Al, C.M.W., Stams, G.J., Bek, M.S., Damen, E.M., Asscher, J.J., & Van der Laan, P.H. (2012). A meta-analysis of intensive family preservation programs: Placement prevention and improvement of family functioning. *Children and Youth Services Review*, 34 (8), 1472-1492.

Garfat, T. & Fulcher, L. C. (2012) Characteristics of a Relational Child and Youth Care Approach. *In T. Garfat & L. C. Fulcher (Eds) Child and Youth Care in Practice.* Cape Town: Pretext Publishing, pp. 5-24.

Garfat, T., & Shaw, K. (2004). From front line to family home: A youth care approach to working with families. In T. Garfat (Ed.), *A child and youth care approach to working with families* (pp. 39-54). New York: Haworth Press.

Garfat, T. (2008). The inter-personal in-between: An exploration of relational child and youth care practice. In G. Bellefeuille and F. Ricks (Eds.), *Standing on the precipice: Inquiry into the creative potential of child and youth care practice* (pp. 7-34). Edmonton, Alberta: MacEwan.

Gharabaghi, K., & Stuart, C. (2013). *Life-space intervention with children and youth*. Toronto, Canada: Pearson.

Hurley, K.D., Griffith, A., Ingram, S., Bolivar, C., Mason, W.A., & trout, A. (2012). An approach to examining the proximal and intermediate outcomes of an intensive family preservation program. *Journal of Child and Family Studies*, 21 (6), 1003-1017.

Kauffman, F.G. (2007). Intensive family preservation services: The perceptions of client families. *Child and Adolescent Social Work Journal*, 24 (6), 553-563.

Maier, H. (1987). *Developmental group care of children and youth*. New York: Haworth Press.

Martin, J., & Stuart, C. (2011). Working with cyberspace in the life-space. *Relational Child & Youth Care Practice*, 24 (1/2), 55-66.

McWey, L.M., Humphreys, J., & Pazdera, A.L. (2011). Action-oriented evaluation of an in-home therapy program for families at risk for foster care placement. *Journal of marital and Family Therapy*, 37 (2), 137-152.

Phelan, J. (2004). Child and youth care family support work. In T. Garfat (Ed.), *A child and youth care approach to working with families* (pp. 55-64). New York: Haworth Press.

Stuart, C. (2009). *Foundations of child and youth care*. Dubuque, NY: Kendall Hunt Publishing.

Tyuse, S.W., Hong, P.P., & Stretch, J.J. (2010). Evaluation of an intensive in-home family treatment program to prevent out-of-home placement. *Journal of Evidence-based Social Work*, 7 (3), 200-218.

Ward, A. (1998). A model for practice: The therapeutic community. In A. Ward and L. McMahon (Eds.), *matching learning with practice in therapeutic child care* (pp. 70-81). London: Routledge.

* * *

Originally published in *Relational Child and Youth Care Practice* (2013), Vol 26(2), pp 29-33

12

Re-Connect

Thom Garfat and Leon Fulcher

We were walking down the street, just the two of us, enjoying the late fall afternoon. It was one of those days
when the sun lights everything in a gentle, slow orange
that warms the heart and offers one thoughts of late afternoon
naps and warm relationships.

We were enjoying each other's company. You know how it is ...
you're connected with a friend, doing something simple, and
somehow it just seems right, like everything is unfolding as it
should. Who knows what we were talking about; we were much
younger then so probably we were, as my mother used to say,
'solving the problems of the world'. Nowadays neither of us is that
ambitious. It is the memory of friendly connectedness in relationship which remains with us today.

As we passed a shadowed alleyway, a large — even looming —
figure stepped towards us bellowing harshly, "Hey, what are you
doing here?"

It startled, and even frightened, us both.

We looked at each other quickly, communicating silently (ah,
the advantages of working together as part of the same team), immediately turned to the looming figure and stepped forward,
knowing that if you run from perceived danger you signal that you
are threatened whereas if you step towards it, you signal interest.
We both believe that signalling interest is better than signalling

fear — which we know is often interpreted as rejection — and that can lead to serious problems. Hey, what can I say, we had worked in child and youth care for years — after a while some of it just rubs off into your everyday way of being in the world.

"Just hanging out," one of us said. Which of us said it really doesn't matter. When you are working as a team, you are working as a team. Two (or more), in a fluid rhythmic connection, interacting with others. One voice, one co-created way of seeing, shared by some silent communication.

The 'looming figure' raised his right hand in a high five suggesting a desire or a willingness to connect. One of us stepped into it, doing the same; the other hung back a little, 'covering your back' as we used to say. As hands met, the slap was resounding, nothing superficial about it — it was a ritual greeting of encounter offered up with enthusiasm.

"Who is this greeting us with such passion?" we wondered.

Neither of us knew at this point, of course. But what we did know was that whoever he was, he seemed to be seeking a connection — an 'in the moment' engagement with us. And that kind of connection suggests 'relationship'. Now you might wonder 'what the heck were they doing being reflective?' but, like we said earlier, being a CYC Practitioner tends to seep into your daily way of living. It becomes characteristic of who you are.

"Hey," the looming figure belched (yes, sorry, but he did belch it). "Don't you recognize me?"

Well, that was a difficult moment for both of us because neither of us recognized the 'looming figure from the shadowed alleyway'. Any time someone says something like 'don't you recognize me' it is likely that he is calling up memories of an old relationship with you. As we ran through our memories hoping to find a connection neither of us landed on a significant or relevant image of previous experience. We were assuming that we must know this person, but neither of us could make the connection.

"It's Colin," he nearly shouted. "From the kid's home! Remember, you taught me how to kick a football."

"Oh, Damn." we responded almost simultaneously, "Colin the Crusher?"

"That's me!" he replied, his huge beam of momentary pleasure shining through the accumulated street grime.

"Damn, Colin! How are you?"

It seems like a ridiculous question, given that Colin had just emerged from the shadows, looking grubby, needing a shower, and reeking of yesterday's drink. But sometimes you just say whatever comes to mind. After all, living in the world like this is not a science.

We both knew who he was at this point — he had changed from the 'looming figure' to an 'old boy' — one of the kids we had worked with years ago — but no longer a 'kid'. Colin was fully grown, fully present and obviously living a life different than we had hoped for him. Later as we talked about it we discovered we had both felt a bit of guilt at that point, feeling that somehow we had failed him; that his 'being on the street' was a reflection of some 'poor work' on our part back in the Children's Home.

"Not bad, man," he replied. "But I haven't played football since the Home. Those were great times, man." Funny how things hold lingering meaning for people. Here we were on the streets wandering along and all of a sudden Colin looms out of the alleyway, shares a memory, and returns us to the Children's Home days. For a moment it seemed as if we were all back there together but then, just as quickly, we were back 'in the now' with Colin on the street.

"Colin? What's going on? Why are you here?" one of us asked. "Last time we saw you, you were on your way to being a teacher."

Now, some might think that was a quick confrontation but the reality is that if you don't 'seize the moment' it may pass you by forever. One of the things we knew from years of working with people was that there is no sense in wasting time. May as well get to the point now rather than wait until later. Just like a moment of connection can happen in a split second, it can pass just as quickly. And the interesting thing is, people often seem to appreciate the directness.

"Ah, well, you know man, life, and my old lady left me, and she took the kids, and then I lost my job and what the hell, next thing I knew here I was. But it ain't so bad, you know. I mean, I got better friends here than I ever had before." That last did come out a little defensively but making the best of what you got is often a sign of lingering resilience.

"Colin, Colin! It's us. No need to try to make it better. What are you doing to change your life now?"

"Nothing, I guess," he replied. "I mean, what's to do and who's gonna help me anyway?" His momentary joyousness had passed and the depth of his sadness was nearly overwhelming. It was as if some dark cloud that had been hanging over him, suddenly consumed him.

Stepping close together, reaching out to grasp Colin's arms, one of us said, "You are, Colin. You are. Starting right now. And we are going to help you do it."

And he agreed, right there, right then. He nodded his head in a kind of willing acceptance, maybe even a grateful acceptance. The old connection, the old memories of 'good times', coupled with his current state allowed him, perhaps, a new glimmer of hope. Past experiences can do that if one can tap into them.

The three of us walked down the street, heading for a shelter we knew of, where people in Colin's situation often found their second chance. When we arrived, we introduced ourselves and began the process of advocacy for Colin. When the shelter worker asked us what we were doing with Colin, my friend answered, "We're just here to let him know he's not alone and to do whatever we can to help him get back on his feet."

After all, as we said later when talking about it, that is what we do.

* * *

Originally published in *Relational Child and Youth Care Practice,* 2011, Vol. 24 (1/2), pp. 199-200

13

Making Humour Meaningful in Child and Youth Care: A Personal Reflection

John Digney

A piece of black asphalt walked into a bar and immediately tried to pick a fight with each patron. One by one they refused and turned away. The bar tender pointed towards a piece of red asphalt and asked, 'go and ask him to fight with you'. The black asphalt turned and in a high-pitched tone said, 'are you kidding me, there's no way I'd fight him ... he's a cycle-path'.

When we write something down all too often it loses some of its impact. Verbally or at least phonetically the words 'cycle-path' and 'psychopath' are quite similar; very different words, very different meanings but they sound similar. This is all part of the incongruent nature of humour and jokes.

Humour as a concept is exceptionally difficult to define, but it can be described as a message whose ingenuity or verbal skill or incongruity has the power to evoke laughter. It is this incongruity that we as child and youth care workers can utilize as a valid approach to working with children and youth.

Incongruity Theory (Veale, nd) suggests that to find something funny we must see the incongruity or absurdity in it. We allow our-selves to be led along a certain path, with certain expectations only have the direction change dramatically when the punch-line is de-livered. It is this 'twist' that we all too often find funny. Likewise, it is this 'twist' that has it usefulness as an intervention. This is the point were we permit a stepping out of 'reality'. This stepping out can create a moment, where 'all that has happened' up to now is suspended, it we are allowed a moment of reflection and question-ing.

The work Child and Youth Care is serious work indeed: We have responsibility to support, nurture and aid in the development of some of the most vulnerable children, young people and their families, people who are experiencing extraordinary pain and suf-fering. With this in mind, it's not surprising that some people find it incongruent that we would talk about using humour as an inter-vention or part of an interaction. Indeed as I am writing this, I am tempted to mention this story or that story, but keep stopping my-self because I wonder if these would seem inappropriate and worry that my work practice may be called into question. How-ever, because I believe we need to explore and give credibility to this, I think that as professionals we need to share stories, discuss the times that we used 'humorous' interventions and perhaps begin to accept that sometimes it is okay to 'step out of the reality' of some situations, explore alternatives and begin to relate such in-teractions and interventions back to how we can use daily life events for therapeutic purposes.

In what feels like a previous incarnation, I worked in a secure programme. One day I found myself standing outside a young per-son's room. Aaron had been 'timed-out' some five minutes earlier for some misbehavior or other and immediately began to 'trash' his room. My allocated role at this moment in time was to observe and ensure he did not begin to self harm. As I stood watching, I attempted to reason with him. As he pulled off pieces of window sill I started by asking him (through a locked door) to think about why he was behav-ing in this manner and in my most composed tone I was asking him to calm down … of course these were all fuel to the fire. After a mo-ment I began to realise that I would better serve Aaron by being quiet and by not being visible to him.

A laundry cupboard was just outside his room and so I decided to open the door of the cupboard to create a screen between us. Beside the cupboard was the clean laundry, returned earlier from our onsite launderette, so being well domesticated I began to put away the laundry whilst ignoring Aaron's shouting and wrecking. As it happened there were some curtains (drapes) among the linen that day and for some reason, best known to my unconscious, I wrapped one of the large curtains around my waist, I wrapped a towel around my head and hung a sock from each ear. As I stood there in my new attire, Aaron fell silent. 'Surely he can't see me', I panicked, 'no he must be having a rest from smashing stuff', or 'maybe he realized he doesn't have an audience', I thought. Then he again began to shout abusively through his door.

In this moment I got to wondering about how would he react if he were to see me like this – acting the goof. Would he laugh? Would he become more abusive? Would the sight of me dressed in this manner be enough to allow me to re-connect with him in some way and help move this situation towards a resolution? 'Right', I said to myself, and stepped from behind my screen.

Well, the shouting stopped, he stared and stared and then said, 'You've gotta be kidding me – and they tell me I'm messed up'. Good point Aaron! After a few seconds of laughing a conversation began and a short while later Aaron 'came back into the programme'.

Over the last 8 years I have spoken internationally at conferences on the therapeutic uses of humour and indeed examined the uses of humour in child and youth care as my doctoral thesis. During this time I have been amazed with feedback from colleagues about how they use humour for 'therapeutic' purposes. Some of the uses identified over the years and written about include the use of humour as a way to; communicate directly or indirectly with youth, 'connect' or re-connect with youth, 'cajole' or 'defuse' tensions. In addition humour can be seen as a way to demonstrate caring, as a way to 'conceal' negative feelings (such as anxiety or fear) and finally as a way to "cope' with challenges and stresses. In this example, I believe I was (unconsciously) attempting to do all six.

I was communicating a desire to change the current milieu. I wanted to communicate to Aaron that I wasn't upset or angry with him, but that I wished for him to 'engage' with me in a different way – in a way that he need not feel any stress or worry, in a way as social equals, able to have a laugh together.

I was also seeking to re-connect with him, for without a connection we are impotent to be able to help. Elsewhere (Digney 2008a, np) I stated that "It is useful to remember that young people often have a great sense of humour and tapping into this can lead to engagement with youth, which in turn may facilitate us in the process of connecting with them". Taking these few moments to consider 'alternatives' or as a colleague once said to me, 'how we can get in through the side-door', often pays dividends. As moments arrive and leave we must consider how to not waste them.

This intervention with Aaron was clearly an attempt to cajole him out of the bad place he found himself. In this context I use the word cajole to mean, 'to encourage or persuade by effort' or 'to coax'. The disarming or defusing effect of humour is immense and in our work with young people, "we can use humour to provide perspective and to help ... deal with the emotional turmoil ... through creating a 'break' in the present giving time to allow a reframing and providing of perspective (Digney, 2008b, np).

I would hope that my decision to make myself vulnerable in this way allowed Aaron see that I cared enough about him. I was prepared to make an idiot out of myself and open myself up for ridicule from all the other kids and staff dressing myself up in this way. "Our connections with clients through humor, love, and pain contribute enormously to our growth as individuals ... and increase our capacity for empathy and understanding" Harvey (2003, np). Elsewhere (Digney, 2005) I stated, "...it [humour] makes it possible to let young people see that you care. Sharing a laugh, for example can be a non-threatening demonstration of empathy and caring...It is often easier for a young person to accept that someone cares about them if it is not explicitly stated and presented in a humorous manner". (p. 12).

I was concealing my concern about how the situation would

progress and hiding my feelings of anxiety about being able to bring some order back into the programme. Additionally I was wanting to hide feelings of frustration and annoyance. This links well to the following point: I was seeking to cope with the feelings associated with Aarons threatening and abusive verbal onslaught.

But more than this, I was attempting to create a different way of 'being with' Aaron, in his life at this time; to create a momentary contextual shift that could 'shock' him back to a place where we could interact in a therapeutic manner. For better or worse, I believe (though somewhat unintentionally) that this particular intervention matches very closely the characteristics associated with a Child and Youth Care Approach (Garfat & Fulcher, 2012) and the principles associated with the use of daily life events for therapeutic purposes.

This interaction occurred by being with a young person as he lived his life. It was an intentional proactive intervention which was developmentally appropriate. The interaction occurred while 'Hanging Out' and 'Hanging In' with Aaron. It was an example of 'doing with', (not for or to) and was based on engage- ment and connection.

The interaction was based in the context of our 'relationship', could be described as having a needs-based focus and was focused on the present. In addition, this was without doubt a flexible and individual approach, with a focus on the context in which the interaction was occurring. I believe that I attended to and used the rhythmicity of the situation, whilst having clear self-awareness and using 'self' and that the entire episode was about the use of daily life events (thankfully not an everyday event) as a focus for intervention.

As with every action, I think we should take some time to reflect, maybe not necessarily to an in-depth level at the time, but to do this sometime. So now after these long years have passed, I come to again consider that interaction and wonder further about that day. I still wonder if Aaron even remembers that event (I certainly know many of my ex-colleagues do) and I wonder if it has remained with him in the same way it remains with me. And why is this something I wonder about? Is this about my concerns over whether this was a professional way to behave?

As I reminisce about that day I like to believe that I remember making informed decisions and as I rewrite this paper (another 8 years later), I wonder about the validity of such a belief. But as much as I reflect on this, I can't help but wonder, whose needs was I trying to meet? Was Aaron not entitled to act out, was this not what he needed to do at that time, did I prevent him from being in an emotional place that was appropriate? In the final analysis, I presented a 'situation' to Aaron and hoped that he would find it amusing and take it as a humorous diversion and I wonder if this way of 'being with' him have any longer term effects on how Aaron now conducts his life?

In the first publishing of this paper some 8 years ago I posed the question, 'who's benefit was it for anyway'. I still have the same question, but am more accepting of the belief that there was a mutual benefit and we each benefited from this brief intervention in that moment. The real question I think must be, 'did I help make this (or any) moment meaningful to Aaron in a way that positively influenced how he now lives his life'?

References

Digney, J. (2005). Towards a comprehension of the roles of humour in Child and Youth Care. *Relational Child and Youth Care Practice*, 18, 4. pp. 9-18.

Digney, J. (2008a). Humour, Relationships and Connection. www.cyc-net.org/cyc-online/cyconline-may2008-digney.html

Digney, J. (2008b). Humour, Relationships and Cajoling. www.cyc-net.org/cyc-online/cyconline-july2008-digney3.html

Garfat, T. & Fulcher, F. (2012) Characteristics of a Child and Youth Care Approach.In T. Garfat, , L. C. Fulcher and J. Digney, (eds.) pp. 12-34 . *The Therapeutic Use of Daily Life Events*. Pretext, Cape Town

Harvey, M.A. (2003). Audiology and Motivational Interviewing: A Psychologist's Perspective http://www.audiologyonline.com/articles/audiology-and-motivational-interviewing-psychologist-1119

Veale, T. (nd) Incongruity in Humour: Root Cause or Epiphenomenon? http://afflatus.ucd.ie/papers/fest2004.pdf

14

'Zoning In' to Daily Life Events that Facilitate Therapeutic Change in Child and Youth Care Practice

Leon Fulcher

Introduction

Therapeutic Use of Daily Life Events with young people in out-of-home care is frequently a policy aspiration of Human Service organizations, often without clear appreciation for what it means to live with, and influence the lives of, challenged and challenging young people during important periods in their lives. The reader here is invited to 'zone-in' on a handful of Child and Youth Care principles (Garfat & Fulcher, 2011) that assist Child and Youth Care Practitioners to enter *'zones of proximal development'* in shared life spaces with particular young people as Carers in designated out-of-home placements. Duty of care obligations and responsibilities impact on a variety of 'zones' that determine whether therapeutic use of daily life events actually provide opportunities for young people to achieve developmental outcomes that matter during their placement(s) in out-of-home care. Implications for practice and supervision of out-of-home care practices are briefly examined.

Principle 1: Participate with People as They Live Their Lives

At Conference Workshops or Keynote Addresses, Henry Maier used to remind Child and Youth Care Workers, Supervisors, and Managers that BEFORE a word gets spoken, the whole Sensorimotor stage of cognitive development has been activated. Maier (1979) further argued that Specialized Behaviour Training with young people is most successful when Bodily Comfort, Differences, Rhythmicity, Predictability, and Dependability components of his Core of Care have been activated in daily life spaces with peers (Smith, Fulcher & Doran, 2013). Maier showed how relationships play a significant role in determining whether a young person achieves developmental outcomes that matter to that young person, and to her or his family members and community. Social capabilities and competencies build upon personal attachments. Nurturing self-management and enriching a child or young person's behavioural repertoires are closely linked to quality relationships with Carers.

Principle 2: Working in the Now

The Child and Youth Care field has become increasingly aware that learning is a social process rather than just, or even primarily, an individual, deep-brain learning process. Social learning happens in groups, or as Maier noted, at the very least through relationships. While contemporary Western psychological theory focused more and more on individual deep-brain learning processes, the Russian psychologist Vygotsky was arguing that learning and cognitive development takes place firstly on a social plane before it is subsequently incorporated into a young person's cognitive schema. Knowledge and meaning are socially constructed by the particular parties involved in the social learning process – teachers or out-of-home carers and learners – rather than information merely transmitted from one person to the other, as more traditional views of teaching and learning might suggest (Stremmel, 1993). Through the assistance of a more capable person, a child is able to learn skills or aspects of a skill that go beyond that child's actual developmental or maturational level, such that development follows the young person's potential to learn.

Principle 3: Doing 'With', Not 'For' or 'To'

From 1926-30, Vygotsky investigated the development of higher cognitive functions of logical memory, selective attention, decision making, and language comprehension. This young Russian psychologist studied three different angles: first trying to understand the ways in which humans use objects as aides in memory and reasoning; second, how children acquire higher cognitive functions during learning; and third, ways in which learning trajectories are shaped by different social and cultural patterns of interaction. A central theme in Vygotsky's work related to what he called the *'zone of proximal development.'* Essentially, children or young people grow and can be supported in their personal and social growth towards the next stage of development through the guidance of appropriate adults or more skilled peers. This *'zone of proximal development'* is socially mediated and is shaped through dialogue and relationships in daily life events in their life space. Adults may be accorded a role as 'more knowledgeable others' in working with children, to help these young people to identify and develop personal and social skills. Peers also play a role in mediating personal and cognitive development, and especially social development (Emond, 2000).

Principle 4: Responsively Developmental

Vygotsky's idea of *'zone of proximal development'* lends itself to working with groups of young people because it is fundamentally social, and also broadly educational rather than individual and problem-focused. It reinforces the importance of relationships and thus provides a robust psychological underpinning for the therapeutic use of daily life events in social education or social pedagogy. Tragically, Vygotsky died of tuberculosis in 1934, at the age of 37, in Moscow, with much of his seminal work unpublished until the 1980s. Building later on the *'zone of proximal development'* idea, Eichsteller and Holthoff (2010) concluded that learning takes place when young people actually leave their comfort zone to explore wider dimensions of their environment, thereby extending their learning zone to the extent that young people review capabilities and extend the potential limits of their abilities. Pushed too far, young people enter a panic zone, where lack of knowledge and understanding – along with resultant anxiety – often inhibits their ability to learn. Alongside young people, Child and Youth Care Practitioners encourage them to step out of their comfort zones and into their personal learning zone.

Principle 5: Intentionality of Action

To create opportunities where young people can engage with optimal learning opportunities, she or he needs to experience a degree of safety and trust in their learning moment. The level of challenge each young person faces must offer a manageable fit with how they view their own capabilities. It is here that their '*zone of proximal development*' assumes considerable meaning in practice. Think of how many times as a Child and Youth Care Practitioner one might have heard a young person say '*I'm in the Zone!*' This may have been around a sporting activity such as basketball or football, or an art, sculpturing, or photography activity! For that reason, Child and Youth Care Practitioners must remain attentive to this other 'zone' where opportunities for learning and achievement of developmental outcomes that matter can be nurtured intentionally. One might intentionally offer and arrange events and experiences that balance the right amount of challenge with the offer of learning opportunities, enabling children and young people to achieve incrementally and at their own appropriate pace and level. Experiences of achieving developmental outcomes that matter provide a relational platform for continuing success. As Powis *et al* (1989) noted, a young person who lacks confidence in all areas of her or his life may just need achievement in one area from which to gain self-confidence sufficiently to shift personal attitudes about her or himself and experience enhanced performance in other areas of their life.

Therapeutic Use of 'The Zone' in Daily Life Events with Young People

Child and Youth Care Practitioners can help children and young people in out-of-home care to explore opportunities where learning isn't a painful or frustrating experience. Carers might begin more directly with what really interests this young person and how – together – might we build on those interests to create realistic and achievable learning opportunities through daily life events we share whilst living together. Young people quite readily and willingly respond to personal coaching activities from a Carer with whom they feel respectfully engaged. This highlights the importance of Child and Youth Care Practitioners connecting pro-actively with each child or young person received into out-of-home care. It means engaging without waiting for that young person to make the first move. In the absence of such intentionality on the part of each Child and Youth Care Practitioner, it is easy for negative peer group cultures to emerge which undervalue education (basic reading, writing, and arithmetic) and survival skills for daily living as young adults. Learning to enjoy and achieve begins through relationships that have personal meaning for each young person. Enjoyment and achieve- ment are not rigid expectations in Child and Youth Care Practice. Instead, enjoyment and personal achievements are natural results when we engage and operate in relationships that build with intentionality through each young person's *zone of proximal development.*

Within such relationships – encountered in the present and unencumbered by past feelings – young people find opportunities to experience themselves in new ways. These new ways of being in their world begin to weave together daily life experiences and personal stories that reinforce themes of competence, mastery, trustworthiness, happiness and, perhaps most importantly, hope (Phelan, 2001). During such moments, commun- ication frequently occurs through the senses and shared experiences in daily living, not simply through words. Child and Youth Care Practitioners may recall times when they engaged with young people through arduous physical activities, such as a long cycle ride or a challenging hill walk. During such times, communication is often non-verbal, based more around presence, relationship, and 'doing or being with'. Such shared experiences offer powerful opportunities for identifying and engaging in teachable moments in this young person's *zone of proximal development.*

Supervision of Carers Working in 'The Zone' with Young People

A variety of 'zones' require consideration in the daily and weekly supervision of Agency Carers and Supervisors seeking to apply this *'zone of proximal development'* idea in their daily work with young people in out-of-home care.

Zoning In: Effective supervisors ensure that Carers are zoning in on what are important responses with young people. Responsive practices that nurture developmental achievements and promote resilience amongst young people in out-of-home cares involves more than reacting to a young person's behaviour, or the behaviours of a group of youths.

Zone Offence: Good supervisors encourage Carers to influence the Personal Care and Education Plan, and to use it as a guide. Responsive practices involve intervening in a planned manner which considers each young person's current developmental stage and needs, and the context which relocated that young person into this out-of-home care placement.

Zone Defence: Thoughtful supervisors encourage Carers to consider alternative Plans B and C so that when one approach doesn't seem to be working, there is always a back-up plan. This helps with responding with each young person placed in out-of-home care in a manner consistent with how she or he experiences her or himself at any moment in time.

*Zone Press:*The more Carers take account of particular developmental requirements each young person brings with them into out-of-home care, the more responsive each Carer will be in their pro-active use of daily life events with that young person. Stay close to that young person and their 'Zone'. This matters throughout that young person's stay in out-of-home care, however short or long.

End Zone: Health and welfare services promote 'evidence-based practices' with children and young people in out-of-home care. Few of these services attend closely to 'practice-based evidence' (Parsonson, 2012). Responsive supervision reinforces 'good enough caring in each young person's zone of proximal development'. The idea is to address the particular developmental needs and achievements that each young person brings with them into out-of-home care, and ensure that they continue to achieve throughout their placement(s)!

Zoned-Out: Attentive supervision picks up immediately when it seems that Carers are not in sync with a young person in their care. When a placement is disrupted or breaks down because of less than expected change, so it is that personal care and treatment plans are commonly amended without any systematic scrutiny of whether there is evidence to show whether this placement was addressing the needs of this particular youth in the first place.

Loading Zone: Any agency which accepts local government commissioning or enters into purchase-of-service contracts to provide out-of-home care, legally accepts a duty of care mandate from the State – through legislation which lays down criteria around which the supervision of each young person in out-of-home placement and their conditions of residence are reviewed (Fulcher, 2000).

No Parking Zone: The duty of care mandate for out-of-home placements offers each child, young person, and family a minimum guarantee not to be harmed or made unsafe through 'as therapeutic as possible' use of daily life events with young people placed with designated out-of-home Carers. No parking zones extend to offices and to hiding away completing administrivia!

Tow-Away Zone: Supervision of each Carer requires regular and also 'as needed' contact so that agencies demonstrate accountability and compliance around issues of personal liability as well as vicarious liability (that which holds agency management liable through failure to supervise) for the duration of each young person's stay in out-of-home care.

Safety Zone: Telephone and on-site supervision can be supplemented through Carer Groups, Peer and Buddy-Supervision, Telephone Ladders, and Team Supervision. Each of the Child and Youth Care Practice principles highlighted at the start of this article also apply in Carer Supervision.

Re-Fueling Zone: Whether by telephone, Skype, or video conference, on-line forums, face-to-face meetings with individuals, couples, foster families or groups and teams of Carers, weekly and monthly supervision needs to review particular accounts of how Carers participated with young people as they lived their lives during recent days and weeks.

Speed Zone: Invite Carers to slow down, share, and reflect upon actual scenarios from recent encounters with the young person(s) in their care, inviting detailed accounts of scenarios when they experienced working in 'The Zone' with this particular young person in the past few days – and how these experiences left the Carer feeling since.

Zone of Proximal Development: Actively explore a couple of examples involving learning moments where this Carer entered 'The Zone' in their proximal attachment role, willingly able to share accounts about 'Doing With', not 'For' or 'To' a youth in their care.

No Passing Zone: Supervision may usefully explore recent stories and concrete examples which show how this Carer demonstrated her or his capacity to engage in responsively developmental caring with the young person in their care during the past seven days. Be specific and don't let key themes slide by as unimportant. This key supervisory theme explores how the Carer has consciously entered, or attempted to enter, this young person's *'zone of proximal development'* with the aim of nurturing learning outcomes.

Restricted Zone: Good supervision explores how much time is spent in an office or with writing up Care notes when opportunities are there for engaging with young people. Supervision helps to nurture and reinforce **intentionality of action** amongst out-of-home Carers. The aim is to instill a duty of care message that 're-active care is a no-fly zone'. Carers thus learn that they are expected to re-frame daily life experiences with young people in out-of-home care into potential opportunities for pro-active learning for life as a young adult. Here the Supervisor is working in each Carer's *'zone of proximal development.'*

Some Closing Thoughts on Comfort Zones

A central premise underpinning the therapeutic use of daily life events involves professional recognition that 'the other 23 hours' (Trieschman, Whittaker & Brendtro, 1969) are every bit as important as the hour of one-to-one counselling or episode of behaviour management training that gets mandated in a young person's personal care and treatment plan. The 24-hour curriculum provides powerful opportunities for learning. That curriculum extends well beyond formal classroom experiences. There is research evidence now showing how the educational attainments of poorer children actually deteriorates and these children start falling behind their peers during school holiday periods, when these children aren't at school and are living in social environments with restricted opportunities. Such deterioration is less discernible during the school term (Alexander et al, 2001). Findings such as these should encourage Child and Youth Care Practitioners to more actively create and nurture learning opportunities in the proximal zone of development for each child or young person in their care. This holds, whether that young person is richer or poorer, and it needs to remain Carers' focus, throughout the course of that young person's life in out-of-home care. Whether a young person is living in foster care, in supervised kinship care, in receipt of after-school care, engaged in a care leaver programme, receiving in-patient hospital care, attending boarding school, or committed by law to a supervised residential group care centre, each young person's *'zone of proximal development'* merits respect and engagement. When Carers aren't 'working in the zone' with young people, it's not surprising to find youths such as these 'zoned out' from whatever Carers are trying to do. Take time 'outside your Comfort Zone' to reflect on how *'zones of proximal development'* – that relational place nearest to our point of connection with a young person – impacts daily in child and youth care work.

References

Alexander, K., Entwisle, D. & Olson, L. (2001) Schools, achievement, and inequality: a seasonal perspective, *Educational Evaluation and Policy Analysis*, vol 23, no 2, pp 171–91.

Eichsteller, G. & Holthoff, S. (2010) *Social pedagogy training pack*, ThemPra Social Pedagogy Community Interest Company.

Emond, R. (2000) *Survival of the skilful: An ethnographic study of two groups of young people in residential care*, unpublished PhD thesis, University of Stirling.

Fulcher, L. C. (2002) The Duty of Care in Child & Youth Care Practice, *Journal of Child and Youth Care Work*. 17, 73-84.

Garfat, T. & Fulcher, L. C. (eds) (2011) Applications of a Child and Youth Care Approach, *Journal of Relational Child and Youth Care Practice*. Volume 24, Numbers 1-2.

Maier, H. W. (1979. 'The core of care: Essential ingredients for the development of children at home and away from home', *Child Care Quarterly*. vol 8(no: pp 161173.

Parsonson, B. S. (2012) The case for practice-based evidence to support evidence-based practice. *Journal of primary health care*, Vol. 4, No. 2, 98-99.

Phelan, J. (2001) 'Experiential counselling and the CYC practitioner', *Journal of Child and Youth Care Work*, vols 15 and 16, special edition, pp 256–63.

Powis, P., Allsopp, M. & Gannon, B. (1989) 'So the treatment plan', *The Child Care Worker*, vol 5, no 5, pp 3–4.

Smith, M., Fulcher, L. C. & Doran, P. (2013) *Residential Child Care in Practice: Making a Difference*. Bristol: Policy Press.

Stremmel, A. J. (1993) 'Introduction: Implications of Vygotsky's sociocultural theory for child and youth care practice', *Child and Youth Care Forum*, vol 22, no 5, pp 333–5.

Trieschman, A., Whittaker, J. K. & Brendtro, L. K. (1969) *The other 23 hours: child-care work with emotionally disturbed children in a therapeutic milieu*, New York: Aldine De Gruiter.

15

Love and the Child and Youth Care Relationship

Mark Smith

It is hard to write about love without finding oneself singing along to songs on the theme. Love has probably inspired more songs and poetry than any other topic. This might suggest that it is central to the human condition. 'I won't stay in a world without love' goes one such lyric. Yet, we often seem to consign those we work with to just such a fate. We are decidedly squeamish about the idea of love when it strays beyond the realm of the family or of normative romantic relationships.

Thankfully, there are signs that writers in the field are beginning to dare speak the 'L' word and to consider what it might mean in the context of 'professional' relationships. One such writer is Keith White, an academic sociologist who also lives in and runs his family's residential community in London caring for troubled children. In a recent book 'The Growth of Love' White (2008) re-claims two words 'love' and 'God' which many might feel have been banished from the child care lexicon. He doesn't actually define love, taking the view that we all have our own perspectives of what love might be. In a journal review of that book I questioned this decision not to define what he meant by love. On reflection, I think he may be right not to do so. When you start to think about what love is, or might be, it isn't clear-cut. Here, I offer a brief and personal exploration of love in its different guises, arguing that it is a central component of any helping response undertaken in the context of caring relationships.

Bringing together 'love' and 'God', as Keith White does, is a reasonable starting point for my exploration. In John's Gospel, Jesus said to Simon Peter, 'Do you love me … 'Feed my lambs.' … Do you love me?, … 'Tend my sheep.' The command to love is expressed in very practical ways, of feeding the hungry and tending the poor. To love, within a Christian tradition or indeed any religious tradition, becomes one's calling .as a human being. In a more contemporary although still religious context, the great Brazilian educator, Paulo Freire (1972) , identifies that calling as *to become more and more human*. Such 'humanization' involves developing greater love for fellow humans, curiosity for learning, and greater awareness of our incompleteness as living beings, all of which might seem to be a reasonable prospectus for child and youth care workers.

Love, for Freire is not some soppy, squishy feeling. It can also be uncomfortable, what he terms an 'armed love' demanding that we take a stance on behalf of those oppressed individuals and groups we work with. To do so can demand courage, the courage to keep going when things get tough rather than giving up or convincing ourselves that we can no longer meet this individual's needs and somewhere else would be better placed to do so, the courage to love, even those who might not seem to be immediately loveable.

So, if love is such a broad and central aspect of what it is to be human then why might it be subject to such ambivalence in professional circles? Some of the responsibility for this might be laid at the door of the philosophers of the Enlightenment. This was the period of scientific and philosophical activity that swept across Europe over the course of the 17th and 18th Centuries. It marked the beginning of the 'modern' period in human history. '*Cogito ergo sum*', declared Rene Descartes (1641), one of the early Enlightenment philosophers, '*I think therefore I am*'. This was a theme picked up by Immanuel Kant (1964), who identified the power of reason as the defining feature of humanity. Human beings were considered to be rational, autonomous individuals. Reason was counterposed with and elevated above emotion as the pre-eminent human goal. Following Kant, rationality became the touchstone of human conduct, notwithstanding the great Scottish philosopher's David Hume's caveat that reason could only be the slave of the passions (2000). Kantian thinking has been particularly influential in the development of ideas of professionalism and professional ethics.

Social work, in its quest for professional status, has embraced modernity's tenets, developing largely around Kantian principles that stress universality, objectivity, reason, legalism and proceduralism (Clark, 2000). Ideas of professionalism have also maintained the reason/emotion dualism, separating out personal from professional selves. This separation is maintained through various 'technologies' such as the use of jargon, the development of competencies, ever more policies and procedures, imposed codes of ethics or conduct, and increasingly, the use of computerised technology borrowed from big business to manage relationships with clients. As 'professionals' we need to maintain a 'professional distance'. Professionals are not to be 'diverted by their personal beliefs and convictions or by emotions – sympathy or antipathy – towards fellow workers or towards individual clients ....'. Actions 'should not be oriented to persons at all, but to the rules ... (Bauman, 1994: 5). We have reached a stage where policy makers and many professional social workers can conceive of a social work that scarcely requires any face-to-face contact at all.

In such a climate, to admit to emotion and especially perhaps to a strong and ambivalent emotion such as love, is dangerous. It will almost certainly provoke a charge of being 'unprofessional'. Of course, this separation of personal and professional selves serves a purpose. It provides a defence against the strong emotions elicited by face to face contact with another. To hide behind a notion of professionalism can be handy when confronted with other peoples' pain, distress, anger or indeed attraction.

There is a problem, however. The assumption that we can separate off our emotional from our rational, our personal from our professional selves is a modernist conceit. More recent philosophical thinking would tend to agree with Hume that reason is a mere slave of the passions. Emanuel Levinas (1969), the 20th Century French philosopher, speaks of us being drawn to the face of the other. He suggests a primary and powerful moral impulse to reach out to them. It is such a call that brings most of us into this kind of work in the first place. But it is impeded by ever-expanding layers of bureaucracy. Levinas advises that in encountering the other we need to do so face to face, without intermediaries. Policies and procedures and the various other 'technologies' that are applied to care act as intermediaries that dull our caring impulse and indeed redefine the caring task away from a practical/moral one to a technical/rational one.

So a tension emerges between a moral desire to reach out to the other in love and the fear of doing so, fear of what others might think, fear that it's not 'professional', fear perhaps of our shadow selves and that we might get too close. All relationships exist, somewhere along this continuum of love and fear. Fear is the greatest inhibitor of human growth; it makes us scared of others and scared to reach out to them. We look to impose intermediaries to our relationships and we call them professional boundaries. More often than not, what we call boundaries are actually barriers. Barriers broach little messiness or ambiguity; they are the *'Thou shalt not'* injunctions beloved of administrators and regulators... *'Thou shalt not drop by on your day off to take a kid to a football match'.* *'Thou shalt not disclose any details of your own personal circumstances to families you want to know every last detail about'.* *'Thou shalt not touch kids.'* *'Thou shalt not invite anyone you ever worked with in a professional capacity into your own home'.* To be professional in this distorted version of professionalism is to surround relationships in fear, when proper, healthy, growth-inducing relationships are characterised by love (see Smith, 2008).

Boundaries, on the other hand emerge from reflection on our thoughts and feelings about the nature of our relationships with others and how close these should be. Should they be at the same level of intimacy with one person as another, and whose interests are really being served here anyway? Effective boundaries require such a journey inwards, to examine our feelings and desires, conscious or otherwise in relationships. This is messy and ambiguous work; intimate relationships are driven by and throw up a range of emotions.

Among the emotions that may creep into our relationships is eros, that element of sexual or sensuous attraction, which, in an act of collective denial, can foreclose any discussion of love in respectable, or at least professional, company. The existence of eros in personal/professional relationships is, nevertheless, inevitable; it is part and parcel of our irrational impulse to care. Fewster (2000) points out that 'sexuality, in the broadest sense, is a powerful and persistent theme that, in one way or another, implicitly or explicitly, plays itself out within and between both participants' (worker and child). Yet, as Fewster goes on to observe, practitioners *'find compelling reasons to place their own sexuality in cold storage when it comes to working with their 'clients.'* (p.8) Sexuality, more so even than other strong emotions, becomes split off from 'self', a situation which is neither conceptually nor practically feasible and one that gets in the way of building authentic personal relationships. For staff in caring roles to engage safely and authentically with those they work with requires a preparedness to explore and accept sexuality as integral to 'self'. Instead, we conflate it with abuse and in so doing we replace one tyranny with another, a tyranny of blandness (Mc William, 2000).

Loving relationships are rarely bland. Nor are they necessarily consensual and cosy. Attempting to teach my daughter to drive brings that point home to me. Close relationships can be fraught and conflictual, and can involve strong negative feelings. But, if they are characterised by a belief that the relationship will endure beyond the difficult episodes, then they will be worked through and come to cement the relational bond. It is the same with professional relationships. There are times that we need to fall out with those we work with, sometime spectacularly, but we need to have the courage to do this at a relational level rather than hiding behind legislation and systems to give people the bad news. And then point them towards some formal complaints system when they aren't happy with what we've done.

In social work in the UK we are increasingly exhorted to take the views of service users into account in delivering services. And when you explore what service users say they want it can be quite simple; they want to be treated with respect – like a friend and an equal (McLeod, 2010). The reality of course is that many professional relationships cannot be thought of as equal – they may involve compulsion and they will almost invariably involve some power imbalance. But inequality need not preclude friendship nor indeed love in relationships. Again, theologians such as Thomas Aquinas offer a far better developed examination of this possibility than the kind of simplistic 'professional' cultures that identify inequality in relationships as inhibiting friendship or indeed love within them.

Now, having stated a case for the acceptance of love as central to relationships I would introduce a caution. While the expression of love becomes more problematic in professional discourse, the word itself has become over-used. This simplifies the depth and complexity of love and reduces it to a Hollywood parody. Sitting on the bus to work I hear all sorts of mobile phone conversations. Increasingly, it seems, rather than just say goodbye, people sign off by saying 'Love you'. I'm not sure what, if anything, it means. Now, my own adolescent sons would never tell their mum or myself that they loved us, nor would they appreciate being told that. But I'm sure they know it to be the case. So it seems to me that people will know what they mean to us, less through what we say than what we do and how we are with them.

As I try and bring my exploration back to what it says in its title I struggle to separate the two elements, love and child and youth care. Child and youth care in contrast perhaps to other professions or aspiring professions is irredeemably a practical, moral and relational endeavour. As such, it is fertile ground for the growth of love. White suggests that love grows in the common things of life – "the daily round and common task; the regular encounters, greetings and farewells, shared experiences...." (p. 206). This is a life space approach, the use of everyday events as they occur to promote growth, not the kind of growth that psychologists talk about and want to measure but the kind of growth that emerges from human connection and relationship. But that relationship needs to be what White calls 'right relationship', governed by the right intentions and competent action. That, in turn, requires practice cultures that move beyond the instrumental and managerial to promote and support reflexivity, organisational cultures that through parallel processes operate from a notion of love rather than fear at their heart.

References

Bauman, Z (1994). *Alone Again: Ethics after the age of certainty* London: Demos.

Clark, C. (2000). *Social Work Ethics: Politics, Principles and Practice*, Basingstoke: MacMillan.

Descartes, R. (1641). 'Meditation VI', in *Meditations on the First Philosophy*. Taken from Stanford Encyclopaedia of Philosophy http://plato.stanford.edu/entries/dualism/#HisDua accessed Dec 2010

Fewster, G. (2000). Morality, Empathy, and Sexuality? *Journal of Child &Youth Care*, 14 (4), 1-17.

Freire, P. (1972). Pedagogy of the Oppressed, Harmondsworth: Penguin.

Hume, DA (2000). *Treatise of Human Nature* (Oxford Philosophical Texts), David Fate Norton and Mary J. Norton (eds.), Oxford, Clarendon Press.

Kant, I (1964) *Groundwork of the Metaphysics of Morals*, New York, Harper Row.

Levinas, E (1969). *Totality and Infinity: An Essay on Exteriority*. Trans. Alphonso Lingis, Pittsburgh, PA: Duquesne University Press. Taken from Stanford Encyclopaedia of Philosophy http://plato.stanford.edu/entries/levinas/accessed 28th Dec 2010

McLeod, A. (2010). 'A Friend and an Equal': Do Young People in Care Seek the Impossible from their Social Workers? *British Journal of Social Work* 40 (3) 772-788.

McWilliam, E. (2000). Foreword in R. T. Johnson, *Hands Off! The Disappearance of Touch in the Care of Children*. New York: Peter Lang.

Smith, M (2008). Loving or Fearful relationships in C. Sharpe, E. Daniel, S. Degragorio, J. Kenny, and A. Vishnja (Eds.) *Love is Enough: Sincerity and Professionalism in the Care and Education of Children and Young People*. Totnes: Abbeyhill Press.

White, K. J. (2008). *The Growth of Love*, Abingdon: The Bible Reading Fellowship.

* * *

Originally published in *Relational Child and Youth Care Practice*, 2011, Vol. 24 (1/2), pp. 189-192

16

It was one of those moments

Thom Garfat

'It was one of those moments...' is a common phrase in English. It is often used in expressions, like "it was one of those moments when the kids were playing happily and..." or "it was one of those moments when everything seemed to come together and..."

In this simple phrase we acknowledge how a moment can be significant and can be the prelude to other important moments. We recognize the potential power of a moment.

'It was one of those moments' – is also a powerful, meaningful, Child and Youth Care inspired moment of helping. Those are the moments we look for, search out, create, and love. For that, ultimately, is the CYC way – watching for, searching for, and creating moments of meaningful intervention with young people, families, adults, and others. But not all moments are meaningful and making a moment meaningful often involves risk-taking and a lot of reflection.

The therapeutic use of everyday life events; making a moment meaningful. Using this moment in a meaningful way to help a young person, or other, reach a goal we have agreed on together. This is the Child and Youth Care way. Using the moment as it presents itself.

Like the following one maybe, but then it's just a Twilight Reflection and, as always, there is no 'truth' here.

It was a Thursday – I remember because I was thinking 'just one more day' until the weekend and maybe a little break. It had been a tough week so far – the staff had worked hard to make sure everything was okay and they had done well. Then, on Thursday night, the social worker called asking to admit Janine to the program.

Janine was 13. She was 'out of control' they said – so we had to take her into the residential treatment centre where I was working. 'Out of control'? What a stupid statement – my guess was that she was totally 'in control' and others could not control her – so she was labeled. In my experience, that's usually how it works. But I was 'on-call' and I agreed she could be admitted to the program.

After she arrived, the staff called me. There was no special problem, they were just concerned given her 'admitting reputation' which was coloured with phrases like 'watch her closely', 'she is a real difficult case', and, the ultimate scare – provoker, 'be careful with her, she can destroy your program!' And then there was the 'softener'; all the adult males in her family had been violent towards her in one way or another.

So, I decided to go in to the program to meet this girl.

Janine was magic! She created and acted on the world in a way that people just struggled to understand. She was passionate, excited, exciting, hostile, rejecting, self-protective, and provocative. She was alive in a way many other kids just aren't. She scared everyone she had met before.

She was not intimated by her intake, she continued to be 'abusive' of everyone, and she refused to be compliant. She was hanging onto herself, I realized as I watched her interact with the staff in the program. She was Janine and was determined that she would continue to be Janine. She was buzzing and they were reacting. She was on top of it all, and loving it. It was wild, but these were great staff.

It was early evening. Supper had not been eaten. Because of the drama since Janine's intake, it had been put on hold for a bit. The menu called for homemade pizza. Chopped food was scattered on the countertop in the kitchen. I knew the staff would get back to it soon, with some of the other kids who, for the moment, were scattered around watching the show.

I watched the staff with Janine. The staff were bouncing around and Janine was the bouncer. They were doing their best – and they were very skilled staff – but Janine had them going. Don't get me wrong, they were hanging in at a time when other teams might have been dragging her to her room. They were just searching to find a way to connect and I suspect having me there (the boss, so to speak) wasn't helping their creativity.

So, I went to the kitchen, surveyed the half-prepared pizzas, and puttered about with the preparations. I could hear and watch what was going on from there, but it was less intrusive. Janine was in the dining room, exercising her power. I was watching her and the staff – she was so skilled at pushing all their buttons – this is not a criticism of the staff. It is just that Janine was so skilled after years of being in the system. She was totally in control of the moment and the staff were scrambling to keep up with her, encouraging her to calm, reaching out. But this time it just wasn't working.

She was so much in control of everything that I decided to try and intervene into the evolving craziness, assuming that the staff would, as they always did, accept me messing in their affairs. If not, we would talk about it later. They had forgiven me before and I felt safe with them.

I called out – loud – to Janine.

"Janine! Come and help me make the pizza."

She stopped what she was doing and looked directly at me. We had not yet really met, although the staff had tried to introduce us when I arrived.

"Fuck you", she screamed at me. "Make your own fucking pizza!"

I put down the plastic knife I was using and walked into the dining room and right into her face.

She took a deep breath when I arrived, looked right into my eyes and said it again, "Fuck you and your pizza". She obviously saw me as 'authority' and was ready to take me head-on.

I wasn't sure what to do at this point – but here is what I was thinking ... *'this is a scared child. A child in tremendous pain. She feels she has just been dumped here. She does not know what to do or how to be. So she is being the only way she knows how to be. Her way of being, right now, helps her to feel secure, like she's in control of her world and therefore can control what happens to her. This helps her feel safe, but it is a false sense of safety, a desperate attempt which maybe even scares her some. She is a child – she needs to be treated like a child with pain and in fear. She needs containment, security, the reassurance that someone, somebody, is in charge here. Only then might she feel the beginning of safety. She is lost and needs some guidance. She needs to experience the strength of an adult who cares. She needs to realize there can be safety here for her. But all of this has to be offered to her in a way that meets her in this, her moment of agony.'*

Hey! We all have to find a way to understand a child before we intervene. My demanding she come and help me with the pizza was just a way of getting her to focus on me and it seemed to have worked. Now I needed to engage her deeply. But to go back to the story ...

"Fuck you and your pizza," she had just said. I was right in front of her.

I breathed deeply, put a stern look on my face and said quietly, "Don't mess with me, child." I let my voice and face soften on the word *child* and let a little smile come to my eyes. "Come and help me make the pizza. We will feed the others. We will connect together and then we will talk".

I could feel the shocked intake of the nearby staff's breath. I had just sounded threatening, even aggressive, in conversation with a child. In my culture the expression 'don't mess with me' is thought of that way and is often used as a form of 'defensive aggression' and the staff knew it. I am sure at least one of them was wondering about how they would write up this exchange for the 'authorities'. Truth be known, if this didn't work, I would be wondering the same thing.

Janine looked at me hard. It was the moment of moments. The moment of connect or escalate. In that moment it was just her and me, everything else had faded away.

"You got any fucking mushrooms?" she spit out.

I almost laughed in relief but, pretending to be calm, I answered. "Yeah, we got mushrooms. Good ones."

You know, there are times, moments, when you take a risk: when you say to yourself 'this may be one of those moments'. When you say to yourself that it is worth the risk to try and connect, in this moment, with this child, knowing that the connection is what is needed. It is not always successful – indeed we often 'blow it', but if we don't take the 'risk of connection' it may never happen. "Do nothing, nothing happens," one of my early mentors used to say.

I like to say to people I work with, "if the situation is difficult, step into it, don't step away from it". Because if we step away nothing will change – we will just be like all the other people – ineffective people – this child has encountered. But if we step-in, something might end up differently. After all, it is only in the in-between between us where we can really connect. But there is risk here of course.

But back to the story. "Yeah, we got mushrooms," I had said.

"Damn good thing," she said and, believe it or not, headed straight to the kitchen. I was so surprised I tagged along like a puppy, although there was a part of me anxious that if she went in the kitchen before me she might have second ideas about what to do with the knife on the counter, plastic or not.

She walked in ahead of me, picked up the knife, looked back at me and said, "How can you work with a crap knife like this. Don't you got any real ones?"

"It is a real one," I said. "But I guess it is different than what you are used to using. There are probably other things here that are different than what you are used to."

Looking at me like I was dumbly stating the obvious, she responded, "Starting to look that way."

Janine and I made the pizzas, fed everyone, and then, yes, later, while the dishes were being done, we sat down and talked about her life. Turned out she cooked well and was a great talker.

Many years later Janine and I had a chance to talk. And, wouldn't you know it, she brought up that moment. Here, basically, is what she had to say ...

"When you came up to me and said 'don't mess with me, child' at first I thought you sounded like my dad who was always threatening me – but then I heard the word 'child' and it sounded so caring – well, loving, actually – that I just wanted you to hug me

– because I hadn't been hugged by an adult in so many years that I couldn't remember the last time. It wasn't just the word 'child' it was the way you said it – like you really meant it. I just kept hearing the word 'child, child, child' like you were repeating it over and over. I know you didn't keep repeating it but it kept echoing in my head. And then when you said we would 'connect', I just wanted to scream 'yes, that is what I want' although I didn't know it then. And I sure wasn't going to tell you that, but for some reason in that moment, I felt you were there for me. I felt like you cared. That I wasn't alone anymore. I just wanted to do whatever you wanted to do. So I went to the kitchen to make pizza because, really, I thought my life was going to change if I made the pizza."

Moments, eh? You just never know what is going to happen. But if you think really – yes, really – hard, and if you try to understand the child who is there at this moment in her own unique context, and if you act based on that understanding there is the chance – just a chance – that you may connect in a meaningful way, in this moment with this child.

Now, don't get me wrong – I am not suggesting we should be this way with every young person – and I do realize the risk in telling this story. Like it seems as if we should just go ahead and 'meet them on their own level' or something like that. That is not the point here – and that is not what happened – so do not bother to flash this story in the face of your supervisor when he or she calls you in and holds you accountable for how you were with a child!

Mark Krueger has taught us all about *'meeting them where they are at'* (e.g., Krueger, 2000) and has emphasized that it is a particular skill of CYC workers. If you read Mark's work, you will come to know that he is not talking about something like 'match their way of acting on the world' – rather he is talking about knowing the child and engaging with her according to your understanding of that knowing. This is not a reactive way of responding – rather it is a proactive manner of engaging.

How we are with children, young people, and others, gives off important messages to them. How we are might say 'I care' or it might convey something else. When I was with Janine in that moment, based on the little I knew about her, I wanted her to feel like someone cared about her. Fortunately, that is the message she seems to have received.

Moments change lives. They are the opportunity for us, as caring professionals to make a difference through being meaningfully different with this child at this moment. The therapeutic use of daily life events (Garfat, Digney & Fulcher, 2012) suggests that if we are conscious, we may just make such a difference, but only if we are reflective in our work.

As for the interaction between me and Janine, well, it was just one of those moments.

And, yes, I did have a lot of explaining to do after it was over.

References

Garfat, Digney & Fulcher (2012). *The Therapeutic use of Daily Life Events (dle) training manual.* Cape Town: Pretext Publishing.

Krueger, M. (2000). Central themes in child and youth care. *CYC-Online*, Issue 12. Available here:
http://www.cyc-net.org/cyc-online/cycol-0100-krueger.html